THE CONFEDERATE INVASION OF
NEW MEXICO AND ARIZONA, 1861-1862

THE CONFEDERATE INVASION OF NEW MEXICO AND ARIZONA
1861 – 1862
by ROBERT LEE KERBY

In the prolonged and bloody struggle which characterized the American Civil War, few people are conscious of the fact that one phase of the immense and desperate conflict was fought to a decisive finish amid the mountains and deserts of New Mexico and Arizona. Had the Confederacy succeeded in its bold plan to take and hold these strategic areas, victory might well have been within its grasp.

California, with its untold riches in gold, and its precious seaports, was the immediate prize of Sibley's invasion of the West. With Arizona and New Mexico already in Sibley's hand, with the northern Mexican provinces teetering toward capitulation, the objective which would have changed the entire aspect of the great struggle came perilously close to realization. The story of how this war within a war was battled out to decisive finish forms the substance of this first book-length study of the Civil War as fought in the West.

Included in this valuable and important book is a roster of regiments, companies and officers participating in every battle and skirmish of this farthest western campaign, including battle statistics.

In *The Confederate Invasion of New Mexico and Arizona, 1861 – 62*, Robert Lee Kerby has fashioned a readable and scholarly work, which covers a phase of American history of highest interest to every person interested in the Great West, and the epic drama of its part in the bloody and prolonged War Between the States.

Robert E. Lee Kerby, despite the southern lilt to his name, was born in the borough of Manhattan, in the city of New York. A graduate of Fordham Preparatory School, and the University of Notre Dame (B.A. 1955, M.A., history, 1956), he stepped immediately from university classroom into the United States Air Force after his Master's degree was conferred upon him.

Westernlore Great West and Indian Series XIII

Edition limited to 2000 copies

The

Domosh

Collection

A Gift

Keith & Shirley Campbell Library
Music Library at Wilson Hall
Frank H. Stewart Room & University Archives

The Confederate Invasion of
New Mexico and Arizona
1861-1862

by

ROBERT LEE KERBY, M.A.
Lieutenant, United States Air Force

WESTERNLORE PRESS ... TUCSON, ARIZONA 85740

Library of Congress Catalog No. 58-14001
ISBN 0-87026-055-3

PRINTED IN THE UNITED STATES OF AMERICA BY WESTERNLORE PRESS

To Mary

PREFACE

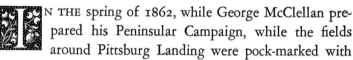N THE spring of 1862, while George McClellan prepared his Peninsular Campaign, while the fields around Pittsburg Landing were pock-marked with bombs and heaped high with the dead of Shiloh, while the *Monitor* and the *Virginia* pounded each other's iron hulls with shot, and while a young Brigadier named Grant rounded up the last of the prisoners from Forts Henry and Donelson, another campaign, all but forgotten by historians of the American Civil War, was being decided on the arid wastelands of New Mexico. Years after the campaign an embittered rebel veteran wrote a commentary which is still a fair evaluation of modern Civil War historiography:

The Eastern Armies had their graphic correspondents, grafted and gifted liars, who magnified mole-hills into mountains and often made a ten-man skirmish a great and bloody battle, where no-one had been touched.[1]

To most of the public and all-too-many historians, the whole Civil War was fought in Virginia and the neighboring states, with but a few skirmishes west of the Mississippi. Jay

---

[1]Theophilus Noel, *Autobiography and Reminiscences* (Chicago: 1904) p. 71.

Preface

Monaghan's recent *Civil War on the Western Border* rectified some of the injustice by showing that Missouri and Arkansas suffered battles just as devastating and a good deal more bitter than those in the east, but thus far no major account has considered the New Mexican campaign worthy of its proper place in the history of the war.

What was its proper place? It was bound more closely to the whole tragic problem of slavery's expansion after 1820 than any other operation of the Rebellion. Since 1820 the South and the North had been drifting apart not so much on the question of the existence of slavery itself, but on that of the expansion of slavery into newly acquired western territories. This was the problem concerned in the most momentous political events of the era: the Missouri Compromise, the Annexation of Texas, the Mexican War, the Wilmot Proviso, the Compromise of 1850, "Squatter Sovereignty," and the Dred Scott Decision. In this light, the New Mexican campaign was not a mere sideshow of the Rebellion. Rather it was the culmination of forty years of domestic political strife in American history, an appeal to arms when words had failed.

In a second sense the New Mexican campaign is also important. Recent military histories of the conflict tend to regard the various "invasions" of the North by rebel armies— even the Gettysburg campaign—as nothing but tactical raids, devoid of permanent strategic value. It is a standard *cliche* that the Confederates lost because they fought a strictly defensive war, without appreciating the value of offensive operations for taking and holding territory. But does an opera-

Preface

tion designed to conquer an area larger than the Confederacy itself, rich in minerals and manpower, and with an immense seacoast that *no* 19th century navy could have blockaded, fit into the pattern? And is the *cliche* true when such a campaign was begun in 1861, early enough to be effective?

A Union officer wrote in retrospect that if the Confederate invasion of New Mexico rendered the conquest of California probable, then it was one of the most decisive campaigns of the war; if the reverse were true, then it was a series of insignificant skirmishes, devoid of military or political significance. But "The capture of Forts Craig and Union [in New Mexico] with their garrisons and supplies would have rendered highly probable the successful accomplishment of the entire plan . . ."[2] Of course this is hypothetical, but the thesis that a rebel victory at Gettysburg would have meant foreign recognition for the South—it could have meant little else—is just as theoretical. And in addition to securing foreign recognition, the New Mexican campaign, as will be indicated, might have won for the Confederacy the gold, men, shipping routes and materiel necessary for victory in the war.

In this volume it is my hope to assimilate the primary sources, some new information, and the best of the few secondary accounts into a fairly detailed military and political history of how the invasion was planned, how it was carried out, and why it failed. I leave the task of fitting the campaign into the general history of the war to others, with the hope

[2]Latham Anderson, "Canby's Services in the New Mexican Campaign," *Battles and Leaders of the Civil War* (1887), II, 698.

xi

that they will consider and apply these facts to a reevaluation of the military and political history of this most terrible of American wars.

Since no books have yet been published about the campaign in general, and since none of the "standard" histories of the war devote much or any space to it,[3] my research has been concentrated primarily on original sources and records, a few published original accounts, and a number of articles in local historical journals by authors interested in particular phases of the New Mexican operation. In spite of an officer's complaint that "Many incidents of great worth to future History have . . . been lost by Deaths, Burning of Trains, baggage, Books, Rolls, papers &c.,"[4] documents are surprisingly numerous, for not only are there the Official Records, but also a collection of Confederate battle reports which includes key records. Diaries, memoirs, and journals are adequate, though, except for a recent edition of the diary of Private Ovando Hollister, 1st Colorado Infantry, all are either unpublished or out of print. The unpublished regimental records of most of the units involved in the campaign are in the National Archives, and those of Confederate units are especially valuable in filling blank spots in the published accounts. The Archives also contain personal letters of participating officers which are not to be found in the Official Records. The sec-

---

[3]The standard one-volume military history, Robert Henry's *Story of the Confederacy*, gives the campaign one-half of one sentence. James Randall's *Civil War and Reconstruction* does not mention it. These examples are typical.

[4]Muster Roll, Co. A, 7th Texas Mounted Vols., C.S.A., Dec. 31, 1862. Old Army Records Dept., National Archives, Washington, D. C.

ondary accounts almost invariably cover specific phases of the campaign; in dealing with them, mine is a problem of co-ordination.

A number of persons deserve my special gratitude. Mr. Elmer O. Parker of the National Archives cheerfully spent hours finding (and dusting off) important documents, and steering me to others. Mrs. Elma A. Madearis of the Museum of New Mexico Library, and Dr. Joan Doyle of the Library of Congress, performed similar services. The staffs of the New York Public Library, the New York Historical Society Library, the Texas State Library (Austin), and the University of Notre Dame Library supplied bibliographical hints and prepared and sent photostats or copies of documents to me; in some instances they led me through bewildering mazes of stacks of isolated, near-forgotten books I could have hardly done without. A number of fellow officers in the Army or Air Force, stationed at San Antonio or El Paso, Texas, checked references in local libraries and newspaper files, and sent copies of documents I could not have otherwise procured. Special words of thanks are due my wife, Mary, who proofread when I would let her and deleted many of my most bewildering sentences and meandering phrases (over my violent protests), and to Dr. Vincent de Santis, of the History Department, University of Notre Dame, who directed my research and without whose suggestions and encouragement it could not have been completed.

This book was originally prepared as a thesis for the degree of Master of Arts, and at the time of writing I enter-

Preface

tained no intention to publish it. Had it not been for the interest of some people I had never met, this book would not have been printed. During a visit to the Shiloh battlefield I happened to mention to Mr. William Kay, Superintendent of the Military Park, that this paper was on file at Notre Dame, and on his initiative he contacted the Military Park Service Superintendent at Fort Union, New Mexico, Mr. Kit Wings. Mr. James Arrott, in charge of publications at Fort Union, assumed responsibility for the manuscript, and he and Mr. William Wallace, Librarian and Archivist of the Rodgers Library, Highlands University, New Mexico, interested Mr. Paul D. Bailey, of the Westernlore Press, in its publication. All of these gentlemen have shown remarkable interest in the work, and no acknowledgment would be complete unless I extended to them my most sincere gratitude.

ROBERT L. KERBY

Sewart Air Force Base, Tennessee
12 March, 1958

xiv

TABLE OF CONTENTS

ILLUSTRATIONS

SHORT TITLE INDEX

(These abbreviations are used in footnotes when one work is cited which contains a number of articles by different authors, or when one author has written more than one article or book.)

B&L: Battles and Leaders of the Civil War (New York: 1887).

Conduct of the War, III p.—: Congress of the United States, *Report of the Joint Committee on the Conduct of the War* (Wash., D. C.: 1863), III, p.—.

Crimmins, "FF" p.—: M. L. Crimmins, "Fort Fillmore," *New Mexico Historical Review*, VI (1931), p.—.

Crimmins, "VV" p.—: Lt. Joseph Bell, "Val Verde," ed. by M. L. Crimmins, *New Mexico Historical Review*, VII (1932), p.—.

MR (followed by regimental number, state, company [if none, it refers to regimental H.Q.], date.): Muster Rolls, —— Regiment, State of ——, —— Company, Date, Old Army Records Department, Room 8-w, National Archives, Washington, D. C.

NMHR: New Mexico Historical Review.

OR: The War of the Rebellion: The Official Records of the Union and Confederate Armies (Wash., D. C.: 1880-1901) (Followed by Series, Volume, Part and Page.).

ORCSA: Official Records of Battles, Published by the Congress of the Confederate States (New York: 1863), p.—.

Twitchell, *OSF*, p.—: Ralph Twitchell, "The Confederate Invasion of New Mexico, Part I, *Old Santa Fe*, III (1916), p.—.

Walker, "Dona Ana," p.—: Chas. Walker, "Confederate Government in Dona Ana County," *New Mexico Historical Review*, VI (1931), p.—.

Walker, "Causes," p.—: Chas Walker, "Causes of the Confederate Invasion of New Mexico," *New Mexico Historical Review*, VIII (1933), p.—.

Watford, "Ambitions," p.—: W. H. Watford, "Confederate Western Ambitions," *Southwestern Historical Quarterly*, XLIV (1940), p.—.

Watford, CHSQ, p.—: W. H. Watford, "The Far-Western Wing of the Rebellion, 1861-1865," *California Historical Society Quarterly*, XXXIV (1955), p.—.

THE CONFEDERATE INVASION OF
NEW MEXICO AND ARIZONA, 1861-1862

CHAPTER I

MAJOR LYNDE LOSES A FORT

EXAS had seceded. Late on the first day of February, 1861, the news flashed over the telegraph wires to all corners of the fast disintegrating Union that Texas had become the seventh sovereign slave state to declare itself independent as a result of Abraham Lincoln's recent election to the presidency. In a few days representatives of the state bearing commissions from the Secession Convention were on their way to Montgomery, Alabama, to assist delegates from South Carolina, Mississippi, Florida, Alabama, Louisiana and Georgia in the formation of a Southern Confederacy. Less than two weeks after their departure the pro-Southern commander of the United States Army in Texas, Brigadier-General David Twiggs, surrendered to elements of the hastily organized rangers and militia of the state nineteen military posts, 2328 officers and men, $1,209,500 in commissary, quartermaster's and ordnance stores, and innumerable horses, mules, wagons, harness, tools and other Federal property, thus virtually confirming the state's withdrawal from the Union. By the end of February armed men belonging to Colonel John Ford's 2d

Regiment, Texas Mounted Volunteers—men wearing uniforms not of the blue cloth so familiar to the civilian population, but of a strange gray—occupied Brazos, Fort Brown and other strategic points in East Texas, while Lt. Col. John R. Baylor's battalion of the same regiment dispersed to receive the capitulations of scattered Union garrisons still in the western parts of the state.[1]

With Texas' ratification of the Provisional Constitution of the Confederate States of America on March 5th, the state militia passed under the jurisdiction of the Southern War Department. On the 16th of March Col. Earl Van Dorn, C.S.A., arrived in San Antonio to assume command of the Department, promptly mustered the state's "army" into federal service, and established more efficient administrative machinery for the reception of Union surrenders. At his direction Col. Henry E. McCullough assumed command of the Eastern Military District of Texas, with headquarters at Tyler, while Col. Ford at Fort Brown retained charge of the Western District.[2]

Baylor's battalion of Ford's 2d Texas was soon ordered to prepare for an expedition to Fort Bliss (El Paso) on the

---

[1]Mrs. C. Baldwin Darrow, "Recollections of the Twiggs Surrender," *Battles and Leaders of the Civil War* (cited hereafter: *B&L*), (New York: 1887.), I, 33, 34, 38-39; *The War of the Rebellion: Official Records of the Union and Confederate Armies* (cited hereafter: *OR*), Ser. I, vol. I, 567-572; Gen. Clement Evans, *Confederate Military History* (Atlanta: 1899), XI, 38-41. Baylor originally organized the 2d Texas, in December '60, as a "buffalo hunting party!"

[2]Evans, *op. cit.*, XI, 44; Gertrude Harris, *A Tale of Men Who Knew Not Fear* (San Antonio: 1935), 10-11. Fort Brown, across the Rio Grande from Mexico, was important throughout the war to the Confederates as a port of entry for military stores purchased in Europe. For short periods it was controlled by the United States Army.

Major Lynde Loses a Fort

state's western frontier, to secure property there and to guard Texas from invasion via the New Mexico Territory and the Upper Rio Grande Valley. Since Fort Bliss was but thirty-eight miles south of an unsurrendered Union fort (Fillmore) at La Mesilla, Dona Ana County, New Mexico, Van Dorn warned Baylor to be watchful and to avoid unnecessary risks, but to be ready to attack Fort Fillmore should a good opportunity offer itself.[3] Van Dorn was then unaware that political turmoil and the collapse of Union military authority in New Mexico nullified the threat suggested by the garrison at Fort Fillmore.

The Territory of New Mexico (the states of New Mexico and Arizona, plus the southern tip of Nevada) was theoretically subject to a government that had been established at Santa Fe in 1850. In actual fact, the appointed executive and the elective legislature, in which the northeastern portions of the Territory were disproportionately represented, were habitually ignored by the southern and western sections. These areas were isolated from Santa Fe by miles of desert and wasteland, and resented the legislature's propensity for concentrating troops around the capital while leaving the rest of New Mexico to the mercies of the dread Apache. As a protest against Congress' refusal to establish a separate government for them, the people of "Arizona" (the present state plus New Mexico below the Jornado del Muerto desert) had established

---

[3] *OR* I, I, 577-578. (Cf. Short Title Index for symbols after "*OR.*")

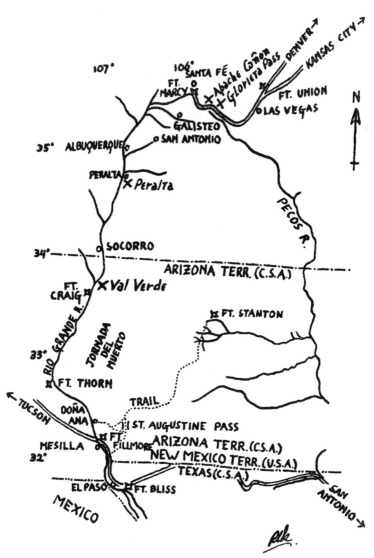

107°
106°
SANTA FÉ
Apache Cañon
Glorieta Pass
DENVER →
KANSAS CITY →
FT. MARCY
FT. UNION
LAS VEGAS
GALISTEO
SAN ANTONIO
N
35°
ALBUQUERQUE
PERALTA
× Peralta
PECOS R.
34°
SOCORRO
ARIZONA TERR. (C.S.A.)
FT. CRAIG
× Val Verde
RIO GRANDE R.
FT. STANTON
JORNADA DEL MUERTO
33°
FT. THORN
TRAIL
TUCSON →
DOÑA ANA
ST. AUGUSTINE PASS
MESILLA
FT. FILLMORE
ARIZONA TERR. (C.S.A.)
32°
NEW MEXICO TERR. (U.S.A.)
TEXAS (C.S.A.)
EL PASO
FT. BLISS
SAN ANTONIO →
MEXICO

FIELD OF MAJOR OPERATIONS
THE RIO GRANDE VALLEY

a *de facto* Territory of Arizona, without sanction, in 1860—before South Carolina's secession.[4]

Economic differences intensified the regional conflicts. While Santa Fe was dependent upon Missouri, Arizona was tied to nearby Texas. When secession became a fact, therefore, Santa Fe preferred to wait and see what course Missouri would follow, while the influential people of Arizona, the merchants, ranchers, miners, lawyers, doctors (and the saloon-keepers and gamblers), called for New Mexico to follow the course of Texas.[5]

Texas, dreaming of expansion and still smarting over the defeat of her claims to the Rio Grande as her western boundary in the Compromise of 1850, looked upon the possibility of establishing a protectorate over New Mexico, or of annexing it outright, as one of the more pleasing consequences of rebellion. On February 4, 1861, Texas passed an ordinance to secure the friendship and cooperation of New Mexico, and delegated Simeon Hart and Phileman Herbert as commissioners to the Territory for the express design of stirring up a

[4]W. H. Watford, "The Far-Western Wing of the Rebellion, 1861-1865," *California Historical Society Quarterly*, XXXIV (1955), 126, 127. (Article cited: Watford, *CHSQ*, p. xix). L. S. Owing, self-appointed "Governor of Arizona" in 1860, claimed jurisdiction below 33° 40'. This region had petitioned the United States Congress for separate organization almost annually since 1856.

[5]*Mesilla* (New Mexico) *Times*, May 11, 1861; Watford, *CHSQ*, 127; E. D. Tittman, "The Exploitation of Treason," *New Mexico Historical Review* cited: Watford, *CHSQ*, p. xix). L. S. Owing, self-appointed "Governor of Invasion of New Mexico, Part I," *Old Santa Fe*, III (1916), 8. (Article cited: Twitchell, *OSF*, p. xix). Though the population of New Mexico in 1860 was 86,793, only a small minority of white moneyed Americans exercised political control.

revolution there. Hart soon happily reported that the people of Arizona were prepared ". . . without a dissenting voice, to join Texas and the South for a Confederacy."[6]

The greatest concentration of Arizona secessionists was in the bustling community of La Mesilla, Dona Ana County, a *depot* of the Butterfield Overland Mail (Stagecoach) Company. Here, in March, 1861, a convention of the politicians and well-to-do from the western and southern portions of New Mexico met and declared that part of the Territory below 34° N. to be under the jurisdiction of the Confederate Government. Within weeks secession leaders were systematically notifying known Union men that it would be healthier for them to move to another climate, and a bright new Confederate flag was brazenly flying within sight of the Union garrison at Fort Fillmore, only three miles away.

Northern New Mexico continued its "wait and see" policy, though H. C. Cook, one of Simeon Hart's agents, reported that the only things holding Santa Fe's secessionists in check were the presence of Union troops and the dependence upon fence-straddling Missouri. Santa Fe ultimately decided to remain loyal, following the hesitant example of Missouri.[7]

---

[6]Wm. Waldrip, "New Mexico During the Civil War," *NMHR* XXVIII (1953), 163n; Evans, *op. cit.*, XI, 22; Watford, *CHSQ*, 128.

[7]Chas. Walker, "Confederate Government in Dona Ana County," *NMHR*, VI (1931), 258. (Article cited: Walker, "Dona Ana," p. xix); *OR* I, IV, 38-39; W. H. Watford, "Confederate Western Ambitions," *Southwestern Historical Quarterly*, XLIV (1940), 164; (cited: Walker, "Ambitions," p. xix). *OR* I, IV, 56-57; Watford, *CHSQ*, p. 128. The southern route of the Butterfield line passed from San Antonio and El Paso via Mesilla and Tucson to Fort Yuma, California. Texas' secession closed it, and in March, 1861, a new route

Major Lynde Loses a Fort

The United States army in New Mexico, struck by one of the worst epidemics of demoralization in its history, was impotent against the rising rebel sympathies. By June the isolated detachments scattered over the Territory found themselves with their pay half a year in arrears, without animals, lacking the ordnance stores and artillery necessary "to arm a single post properly," with their numbers (14 companies) weak and scattered in half a dozen different posts, without any news of the events back East (the secession of Texas closed the Overland line), and faced by a new Apache menace—the Indians, having become convinced that they were the cause of the white men's troubles, came down from their mountain strongholds to drive the "longknives" forever from their hunting grounds. Worst of all, "We were being deserted by our officers ... We were practically an army without officers."[8]

Had the Union officers done their duty as long as they held their commissions, much of the problem would have been temporarily alleviated. But, because of Southern birth or ancestry, or because of the activities of such men as Simeon Hart, who offered promises of pay and promotion in the rebel service, many abandoned their posts to go South, and as a consequence discipline and morale fell apart. Even the Departmental Commander, Col. William W. Loring, took "the Texas route" after his plot to turn everything over to the

was opened further north. The Pony Express offered the only other transcontinental communication until telegraph lines were completed in October, '61.

[8]Walker, "Causes of the Confederate Invasion of New Mexico," *NMHR* VIII (1933), 91 (cited: Walker, "Causes," p. xix) ; Lewis Roe, "With Canby at Valverde, N.M.," *The National Tribune* (Washington, D.C.), Nov. 3, 1910.

rebels was disclosed to the loyal commander of Fort Stanton, Lt. Col. Benjamin Roberts, by a drunken officer.[9]

The problem of demoralization was especially pressing at Fort Fillmore, because most of the deserting officers passed through on their way to Texas, and while there did little to hide their intention to join the rebels. A soldier of the 7th Infantry remembered seeing the late commander of Fort Union, Major Henry Hopkins Sibley, lean from a wagon full of deserting "brass" and yell to some men nearby, "Boys, if you only knew it, I am the worst enemy you have."[10]

Known to the army chiefly as the inventor of the standard "Sibley tent" and "Sibley stove," Major Sibley was a man of some military talent who enjoyed a generally good reputation. His men liked him as a commander who kept a good post without depending too much on regulations, and his fellow officers respected his ability to maintain friendly communications with the usually hostile and always suspicious Indians. His twenty-two year career in the army might have been brilliant, but for the fact that his love of intoxicants alienated some of his superiors. Looking for greener pastures, he resigned his Federal commission on May 13th, tendered his services to the South, and three days later was wearing the

---

[9]U. S. Congress, *Report of the Joint Committee on the Conduct of the War,* (Washington: 1863) III, 366 (cited: *Conduct of the War,* III, p. xix) ; *Ibid.,* 365. Cf. also *OR* I, I, 604 and 599, where Loring urges the U.S. to ship New Mexican garrisons to the eastern front while admitting he has not enough men to hold New Mexico.

[10]Watford, "Ambitions," 165; Roe, *loc. cit.,* J. D. Howland, "On Gory Field Glorieta Heights," *Santa Fe New Mexican,* Aug. 7, 1906.

Major Lynde Loses a Fort

two stars of a Lieutenant-Colonel of Infantry, Confederate States Army.[11]

Arriving at Fort Bliss soon after his resignation, Sibley dispatched many letters to other officers still in New Mexico, including Col. Loring, inducing them to "go South." The letter to Loring was sent a day too late, however, for he had already resigned in favor of Colonel Edward R. S. Canby, one of the few loyal officers left in the Territory. Canby intercepted Sibley's letter and immediately ordered the commander at Fort Fillmore, Major Isaac Lynde, to place Loring under arrest as a traitor, but Lynde reported that Loring had already passed safely into Texas.[12]

Upon assuming command in New Mexico, mild but resolute Colonel Canby found his army falling apart around him. Immediately he set about the near-impossible task of rectifying the situation. When, in late June, intelligence reached him that a body of rebels was massing at Fort Bliss, he warned his superiors in Washington of the danger and started con-

---

[11]Jay Monaghan, *Civil War on the Western Border* (Boston: 1955), 228, 232, 168-169; T. Noel, *Autobiography and Reminiscences,* (Chicago: 1904), various places; Wm. Whitford, *Colorado Volunteers in the Civil War* (Denver: 1906), p. 33; Sibley Jacket, Confederate Archives, Chap. 1, File 88, p. 86, National Archives, Washington, D. C. (Sibley's commission). Like many ex-Federals he was commissioned directly into the Confederate States Provisional Army, equivalent to the United States Regular Army.

[12]F. S. Donnell, "The Confederate Territory of Arizona," *NMHR,* XVII (1942), 151-152; *OR* I, IV, 55-56, 57; *OR* I, I, 606; Watford, "Ambitions," 164. Canby had gained little recognition, though he served honorably in the Mexican War. Very plain-appearing, he was self-possessed, courageous and prudent.

Sibley's letter to Loring incriminated both of them, as well as Simeon Hart, Judge J. F. Crosby, and "Colonel" James Magoffin, an El Paso merchant.

Edward R. S. Canby   BRIG · GEN. U.S.A.

centrating his command at key points along the Rio Grande.
It was most imperative that Fort Fillmore be held until the
garrisons from Forts Breckenridge and Buchanan, in western
Arizona, could be evacuated and brought to reinforce the
troops along the river. Fillmore guarded the only route from
Tucson to eastern New Mexico, and therefore if it fell too
soon the commands at Breckenridge and Buchanan would be
cut off and probably lost. Canby agreed with Major Lynde that
"this post . . . [is] not worth the exertion to hold," but Fillmore had to be held until the soldiers in the western posts
were safe.[13]

In spite of Canby's sound reasoning, Lynde continued to
protest. With the Stars and Bars flying three miles away, and
with deserting officers demoralizing his command, "he had no
confidence that his men would fight." With its commander in
such a frame of mind, it is surprising that Fort Fillmore did
not surrender sooner.[14]

Meanwhile, in the first week of July, Baylor's battalion of
the 2d Texas (Companies A, B, D and E) and Captain Trevanion T. Teel's Battery B, 1st Texas Artillery, occupied El

---

[13]Ovando J. Hollister, *Boldly They Rode*, 2 ed. (Lakewood, Colo.: 1949),
101; Watford, "Ambitions," 164; Watford, *CHSQ*, 128; *OR* I, IV, 58, 45-46,
63-64.

[14]M. L. Crimmins, "Fort Fillmore," *NMHR*, VI (1931), 330 (cited:
Crimmins, "FF," p. xix); *Conduct of the War*, III, 366; *OR* I, IV, 56-57.
Lynde, in spite of Canby's orders, did nothing whatever to reinforce the works
at Fort Fillmore or to improve either the morale or effectiveness of his command. He continued to quarter Southern officers on the post while they awaited
their dismissals. Lynde was a loyal Union man, but incompetent in this situation. He was cashiered the following November, though reinstated after the
war.

Paso and took quarters in Fort Bliss. Soon Baylor was busy collecting every available scrap of information about Fort Fillmore, including details like the size of the guns at the post (twelve-pounders). Soon detachments of his 258-man command were making demonstrations against the position, and on one occasion drove off forty-one horses from the dwindling post herd. Finally convinced that Fillmore was ripe for an assault, Baylor marched on Mesilla on the 23d-24th of July. Aware of the Confederates' approach, Lynde packed all his surplus supplies for shipment to Canby's headquarters at Fort Craig (on the Rio Grande, halfway between Mesilla and Albuquerque), but made no effort to strengthen his own defences. In fact, most of his garrison was asleep when Baylor's Texans occupied Mesilla late on the 24th.[15]

A demand for Baylor's surrender and an abortive attack by the Federals on the afternoon of the 25th hardly disturbed the Confederate recruiting service, which was wining, dining and cajoling many of the local citizens into the Southern regiment with pleasing facility. Finally sure that he had no chance of success, Lynde fired the military stores at Fillmore during the evening of the 26th, looked the other way while his men filled their canteens with medical whiskey, and marched his wobbly-legged companies toward presumed sanctuary at Fort

---

[15]Muster Rolls, 2d Texas Cavalry & 2d Texas Field Battery, National Archives (cited: *MR*); *OR* I, IV, 17; G. H. Pettis, "The Confederate Invasion of New Mexico and Arizona," *B&L* II, 103; Letter, Baylor to Van Dorn, July 17, 1861, Baylor Jacket, National Archives; Crimmins, "FF," 330-331. During the evening of the 24th Baylor tried to assault Fillmore, but a deserter from the Confederates, an ex-Union Regular, warned Lynde in time for him to man the walls. At the time the Confederates were but 600 yards away.

Stanton in such haste that he forgot the post flag. Dawn disclosed to Baylor a pillar of smoke rising over the fort and a cloud of dust disappearing into the east. Quickly forming 162 men of his battalion, he gave chase. Drunk stragglers surrendered all along the road, and by the time the Confederates reached San Augustine pass, twenty miles from Mesilla, almost all of Lynde's 400 Regulars were prisoners. During the entire march, not a shot was fired.[16]

Carting the prisoners who were in no condition to walk back to Mesilla in wagons, Colonel Baylor sobered them up and induced a few to enter his regiment. To the rest he offered paroles, a precedent followed by the usually impoverished armies of both sides during the rest of the New Mexican campaign. Though eighteen preferred to be bound only by wooden stockades rather than by their words of honor, most accepted the paroles.[17]

Baylor soon found how little the East knew of the operations around Dona Ana. At Fort Fillmore he captured $9,500 in Federal drafts, and succeeded in cashing $4,500 drawn on the assistant United States treasurer at New York before the Union government realized that Fillmore had become the property of the Confederacy![18]

---

[16]Hank Smith, "With the Confederates in New Mexico," *Panhandle-Plains Historical Review,* II (1929), 70-72, 77, 78; Crimmins, *"FF,"* 331, 332; Watford, *CHSQ,* 130.

[17]Smith, *op. cit.,* II, 79, 80; Aurora Hunt, *The Army of the Pacific* (Glendale, Calif. 1951), 53; Roe, *loc. cit.*

[18]OR I, IV, 157-158. A summary of the Fort Fillmore "battle" and surrender appears in *OR* I, IV, 14, 16-20. Lynde, the officers' families, and a troop of men escaped capture at San Augustine Pass.

The Confederate Invasion of New Mexico and Arizona

A few weeks after the *debacle* at Fort Fillmore a company of Confederate Arizona volunteers, while chasing a band of renegade Apache, stumbled on the garrisons from Forts Breckenridge and Buchanan on the Mesilla-Tucson road. The Federals had razed and abandoned their posts under orders from Canby and, still unaware that Fillmore had surrendered, were on their way to Fort Craig via Mesilla. The Arizona scouts, "taking notes on everything," prepared an ambush at Picacho (a day's march west of Mesilla) with the help of reinforcements from Baylor, and waited for the Nationals to fall into it. The Federals were already in Cook's Cañon, a short distance off, when their commander, Capt. Isaac Moore, received word of Lynde's fate from Colonel Canby. In a few short minutes Moore fired his wagons and struck out over the Jornado on a seventy-five mile desert hike to Fort Craig, thus avoiding the trap and saving his four companies for later campaigning.[19]

As a result of the general collapse of Union military authority in Dona Ana, Lt. Col. Roberts destroyed Fort Stanton and withdrew his garrison to Craig. His evacuation left the entire southern half of the Territory in the Texas battalion's control.[20] Its reconquest seemed impossible, for Canby had but 2,466 men with whom to hold what he had, and was

---

[19]Smith, *op. cit.*, 81-89; Watford, "Ambitions," 166; R. K. Wyllys, "Arizona and the Civil War," *Arizona Highways*, XXVII (1951), 34; Pettis, *op. cit.*, II, 103. The Arizona scouts were nineteen men of Tom Helm's company under Lts. Sutherland and Jackson.

[20]Pettis, *op. cit.*, II, 104; Watford, "Ambitions," 166. Roberts' garrison was composed of elements of the 3d United States Cavalry.

isolated in a desert without funds, provisions, mounts, uniforms, guns, ammunition and officers. In spite of this, and in spite of the general demoralization of his regiments, the dedicated Colonel was to double the size and square the effectiveness and morale of his command by the end of the year. In addition to begging Washington for reinforcements he secured authority to raise four regiments of New Mexican volunteers for three year terms. When, by the end of September, New Mexico had produced only fourteen ill-equipped companies (only one of which was cavalry) for terms as short as six months, he requested William Gilpin, Governor of the Colorado Territory, for men to garrison a last line of defence at Fort Garland, Colorado. In this Canby was exceeding his authority, but the security of New Mexico demanded boldness.[21]

The lack of money and supplies plagued Canby. His mounted volunteers were obliged to provide their own horses, accoutrements and harness without receiving the pay of cavalrymen, but only forty cents a day "for their [horses'] use and risk." All recruits were expected to buy their own uniforms, but the pay for the Regulars, who were most in need, was eight to twelve months in arrears. Even when a man was able to buy a uniform (and whole companies could not), he usually found it to be shoddier than the clothes of Mexican peons.[22]

---

[21]*OR* I, III, 301; *OR* I, IV, 53, 69-70; *OR* III, I, 775; Twitchell, *OSF* III, 16. The four regiments were to be two each of cavalry and infantry. Canby also talked Congress out of shipping his Regulars to the Eastern front.

Until the early spring of 1862, Canby did not once receive a word of praise or encouragement or a promise of reinforcement from his superiors in Washington. In 1862 Col. Roberts testified to a Congressional Committee that Major-General Lorenzo Thomas, the Adjutant-General of the United States Army, was "not gratified at [the New Mexican troops'] loyalty and their successes in saving that Territory for the Union."[23]

The lack of officers was especially disturbing. Even if Canby could raise all the troops he wished he had not one Regular officer to spare for them, and as a result he was obliged to brevet, without any authority, many sergeants to commissioned rank. Though all of these men served honorably and some heroically, they were never recognized or paid by the War Department according to their service.[24]

In August, Canby organized his scattered volunteers into two regiments, the First and Second New Mexico Volunteers, commanded by Colonels Christopher "Kit" Carson and Miguel Pino, respectively. These regiments, in turn, were brigaded under Colonel Roberts. Though only skeleton units at first, their ranks filled as the year waned.[25]

---

[22]*MR* 1st N. M., Co. A (May 31, 1862), Co. G (Sept.-Oct., 1861), Co. H (Sept.-Dec., 1861); *Conduct of the War*, III, 370. Almost all the departmental paymasters had gone to Texas, taking their funds with them. Regular cavalrymen also received 40c *per diem* for their government-owned horses, in addition to (theoretically) higher pay than the infantry and volunteers.

[23]*Conduct of the War*, III, 370. Thomas, of course, was busy with the war back East—Missouri, Tennessee and Virginia.

[24]*Ibid.*, 369.

[25]MR 2nd N.M., H.Q. (Sept.-Oct., 1861); MS Special Order, no number, Aug. 3, 1861, Carson Jacket, National Archives; *Conduct of the War*, III,

Major Lynde Loses a Fort

While in the process of organizing an army, Canby started "playing the war by ear." He reasoned that there were two ideal invasion routes opened to the Confederates, both of which concentrated on Santa Fe. One was by way of El Paso and the Rio Grande, and its approaches were already controlled by Baylor's battalion at Mesilla. The other entered central New Mexico from the northern Texas panhandle via the Canadian and Pecos rivers, and Canby had uncertain intelligence that a rebel expedition under Van Dorn was preparing to march on Santa Fe by this route. To secure central and northern New Mexico from the Confederates, Canby could either scatter his army in many small detachments along the frontier or concentrate all of his men at a few strategically located strong points guarding the most probable lines of enemy advance. Since dispersion would mean defeat in the face of massed Confederate armies, Canby selected two key forts upon which to build his defence: Fort Craig on the Rio Grande, to hold Baylor in check, and Fort Union near the Pecos, to plug the route from North Texas.[26]

Once a few temporary earthworks were thrown up round-about, Fort Craig was considered adequate for defence. But

---

366. One of Canby's officers, Capt. James "Paddy" Graydon, actually impressed Mexican peons into his "Spy (cavalry) Company" in order to bring it to and keep it at full strength.

[26]Watford, "Ambitions," 171; Whitford, *op. cit.,* 34; L. Anderson, "Canby's Services in the New Mexican Campaign," *B&L* II, 698. In actual fact the alleged Van Dorn expedition, though contemplated by the Confederates, was not carried out, as it became necessary to divert Texas troops to the army of Gen. Sterling Price, campaigning in Missouri and Arkansas. Canby did not learn this, however, until later in the fall of 1861, by which time the new Fort Union already presented a formidable facade.

Fort Union, a mere Indian-country stockade, was in no condition to withstand siege by a trained white army, and therefore Canby dispatched five companies of his New Mexican Volunteers, under Lt. Col. Gabriel R. Paul, with orders to build an entirely new fort near the old site. Disregarding poor equipment and poorer morale among his troops, Paul had the new Fort Union well on its way to completion by October, at which time he was able to release some of his companies for duty back at Craig or elsewhere along the Rio Grande. Canby had since learned that the Confederates planned no invasion along the Pecos route and felt justified in ordering the New Mexicans back to Craig or to a string of light, secondary works Col. Roberts was throwing up near Albuquerque, but his concern for Fort Union was to contribute, eventually, to the expulsion of the Texans from New Mexico.[27]

Canby was then unaware that certain events in far-off California, events which were to measurably assist the Union cause in the Southwest, were occurring simultaneously with those in New Mexico. After the defection of the commander of the Department of the Pacific, General Albert S. Johnston, California secessionists had organized in many of the southern counties and, while making preparations to receive a Confederate army of liberation, had raised the cry of rebellion. Their

---

[27]Pettis, *B&L* II, 104; Whitford, *op. cit.*, 34; *MR* 1st N.M., Cos. A & B (July-Aug., 1861), C July-Oct., 1861), D & F (Sept.-Oct., 1861), D (July-Dec., 1861); *Conduct of the War*, III, 367; Twitchell, *OSF* III, 17-18. Canby preferred Regulars for active service, and so sent New Mexicans to Union, where the danger was less acute. He built the lesser works at Albuquerque (and improved Fort Marcy, at Santa Fe) to secure communications between Fort Craig and the States, via Fort Union and the Santa Fe Trail.

sentiments were encouraged when the sixty-eight voters of Tucson, Arizona, in the summer of 1861, passed an ordinance of secession and delegated a commissioner to the Confederate Congress. Though the citizens of Tucson, in a protest against Canby's removal of troops from Forts Breckenridge and Buchanan, were merely trying to secure protection from the Apache and lawless desperados from any available government, their action in fact did bring the border of the Confederacy flush against that of California. Greatly encouraged, secessionists in California became progressively more brazen in anticipation of the day that the Stars and Bars would flutter over the Pacific coast.[28]

General E. V. Sumner, Johnston's successor, realized that inaction on his part would only contribute to the loss of Southern California. Hastily he organized and sent expeditionary forces from Sacramento with orders to disband companies of rebels drilling in the southern towns and camps, and to garrison Fort Yuma, which guarded the Colorado River crossing of the road to Tucson. By September Sumner had the state under control and had blocked emigration to the Confederate States. But the fire of secession still burned in many hearts.[29]

---

[28]*OR* I, L, pt., 623, 610-611; Wyllys, *op. cit.,* XXVII, 34; J. F. Santee, "The Battle of La Glorieta Pass," *NMHR* VI (1931), 68.

[29]*OR* I, L, pt. 1, 610-611, 773, 603, 691. A laconic one-line General Order from Sumner expressed his determination to hold California: "No Federal troops in the Department of the Pacific will ever surrender to the rebels." (Sept. 3, 1861; *OR* I, L, pt. 1, 603.) To block emigration to Arizona and invasion from there Sumner moored all the boats on the Colorado on the west bank, under guard.

The Confederate Invasion of New Mexico and Arizona

When General David Wright replaced Sumner in the fall of 1861, his immediate problem was not the suppression of California rebels, but the reopening of overland communications with the eastern states. When the southern Butterfield route was blocked by the rebellion of Texas, a temporary northern route through Utah and Colorado was established, but as winter approached it became obvious that this route could not be permanently maintained. With authority from President Abraham Lincoln, Wright started mustering a brigade of California Volunteers, under Colonel James Henry Carleton, for service along the Overland road through New Mexico. During the rest of 1861 these recruits not only prepared for the long desert trek ahead of them, but also became an increasingly effective instrument for the suppression of sporadic, less frequent outbursts by the native California rebels.[30]

While Union armies to the north and west organized and increased in strength, Col. Baylor consolidated his military conquest of Dona Ana by introducing a semi-civil government for the "Confederate States' Territory of Arizona." On August 1st, 1861, a proclamation over his signature declared that portion of New Mexico below 34° N. to be a Confederate

---

[30]Clarence C. Clendenen, "General James Henry Carleton," *NMHR* XXX (1955), 35; Hunt, *op. cit.,* p. 107; Watford, *CHSQ,* 136. While in Southern California Carleton's men also helped allay fears that the rebels would invade the state by crossing Sonora.

Prior to his appointment to this position, Carleton was commander of the Military District of Southern California.

The authority to raise California troops came to Sumner, but Wright was the first to use it effectively (*OR* I, L, pt. 1, 543).

territory with its capital at Mesilla. A quasi-civil judiciary, partially composed of Confederate officers and partially of men left by the Union *regime,* was established, while executive authority was retained by self-appointed Governor Baylor and the "army" which he commanded. Baylor was careful to reserve ultimate authority for the imposition of a civil government on Arizona to the Confederate Congress.[31]

The amazing thing about Baylor's administration was that it was functioning well within a week. The territorial courts, hearing some old and some new cases, sat for two regular sessions and a number of special sessions during the rest of the year. In fact, the courts worked smoothly well into 1862, until the Confederate army's hold on the territory began to weaken. When that happened, the entire Confederate civil government for the Territory disintegrated.[32]

But in the bright days of 1861 Baylor was able to report to Col. Van Dorn, with justifiable pride:

I have established a provisional government for the Territory of Arizona, and made the appointments to fill offices necessary to enforce the laws. I have proclaimed myself governor, have authorized the raising of four companies to hold the territory, and afford protection to the citizens . . .

I have acted in all matters . . . entirely upon my own responsibility . . .[33]

Also to Baylor's credit was his commissioning of J. A. Quinterro as his agent to the Mexican states of Chihuahua and Sonora. Quinterro was charged to collect and transmit ac-

[31]*OR* I, IV, 20-21; Walker, "Dona Ana," 256-261.

[32]Walker, "Dona Ana," 256-261 *et post.*

[33]*OR* I, IV, 23. This letter is dated August 8, 1861.

curate and minute information regarding the population, area, farming potentiality, mineral resources, commercial possibilities, and the extent and state of industry in the two northern Mexican provinces. Evidently Baylor was beginning to realize that his invasion of New Mexico, originally conceived as a simple tactical operation to defend the Texas border, had strategic implications that might make New Mexico the key to Confederate possession of the entire Southwest as far as the Pacific coast.[34]

Unknown to Baylor, Lt. Col. H. H. Sibley, with the blessings of Hart, Crosby and other El Paso rebels, had long since left Texas to go to Richmond and introduce to President Jefferson Davis the arguments for a full-scale invasion of New Mexico.[35]

[34]*OR* I, IV, 22-23; Walker, "Causes," *op. cit.,* 83; Watford, *CHSQ,* 131. In less polite terms Quinterro was a spy; his inquiries were "unofficial."

[35]Watford, "Ambitions," 164. Many Texans wrote Confederate officials, including Davis and the Texan Postmaster-General, Reagan, in favor of a full-scale invasion. Sibley was representing some of these men on his mission, though doubtless his own expert knowledge of the Territory let him develop and perfect many of his arguments with little outside assistance. The arguments, primarily Sibley's but including those of his associates, appear in the second chapter.

General   Adjt & Inspr Generals Office
                 Richmond Va July 9th 1861
                      General H. H. Sibley under instruc-
tions from the President is to proceed to Texas,
there to carry out, in concert with yourself, certain measures, of which he will advise you upon
his arrival at San Antonio — It is desired that
you will extend every facility to General Sibley
in successfully carrying out his instructions,
supplying as far as possible, the materiel for the
armament & equipment of his command and
such needful supplies as he may require
from the different departments under your
control   I am Sir Respy
To   yr Obt Servt
Maj Genl Earl Van Dorn   S Cooper
Comdg San Antonio   A & I G
          Texas

SIBLEY'S LETTER OF INTRODUCTION
TO EARL VAN DORN

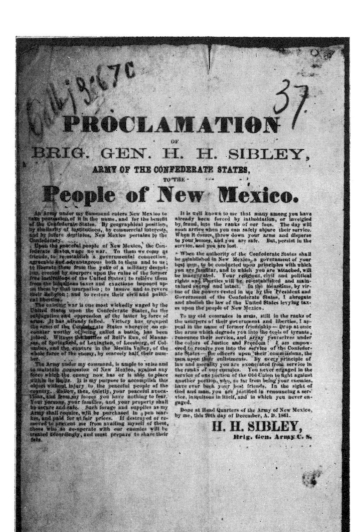

SIBLEY'S PROCLAMATION
DECEMBER 20, 1861

CHAPTER II

GENERAL SIBLEY WINS A COMMAND

IBLEY, with the dream of a Confederacy extending from sea to sea between 26° and 36° N. glittering in his mind, conferred with President Davis a number of times during the month of July, 1861. During these discussions he summarized the many arguments in favor of a major military operation in New Mexico, and gradually persuaded Davis to grant him an independent command for a campaign in the Southwest.

Sibley's arguments were well considered. In the first place, the Southwest offered the Confederacy a gigantic recruiting ground. From its population of 86,000, New Mexico itself could field a small army. Rebels in California corresponded that "if an army of Texans, three thousand strong, were sent to Tucson, Arizona, . . . they would have ten thousand [California] men there with all sorts of provisions . . ."[1] Governor Gilpin of Colorado reported to Washington that "a strong and malignant secession element" had been organized there, and that "extraordinary measures" were required to "meet

---

[1]Noel, *op. cit.*, 56.

and control its onslaught."[2] Mormon Utah was still bitter about its treatment by the United States, and seemed to be "on the eve of a revolution."[3] In short, as a rebel officer later wrote, "there were scattered all over the Western States and Territories Southern men who were anxiously awaiting an opportunity to join the Confederate Army."[4]

Supplying recruits would not be difficult for, as one citizen testified, "The stores, supplies and munitions of war within New Mexico and Arizona are immense."[5] Before the South's secession Secretary of War John Floyd sent much ordnance and small arms to *depots* in the Southwest, and at the time it was estimated 6,000 to 8,000 stands of rifles and twenty-five or thirty cannon were in danger of capture by the Texans.[6]

The conquest of the Southwest would provide ground for the further expansion of slavery—the old argument of Southern Manifest Destiny translated into military terms. Of course, the barren deserts of New Mexico would offer little to the slavocracy, but fertile California would be ideal for the plantation system.[7]

Arizona might also be the springboard for Southern expansion into Old Mexico. With the turmoil of Benito Juarez' *re-*

[2]Whitford, *op. cit.*, 38-39. A riot occurred in Denver when a Confederate flag appeared over Wallingford and Murphy's General Store.

[3]Waldrip, *op. cit.*, 167; *OR* I, IV, 129; Anderson, *op. cit.*, II, 698.

[4]T. T. Teel, "Sibley's New Mexican Campaign," *B&L* II, 700.

[5]*OR* I, IV, 96 (M. H. MacWillie to Davis, June 30, 1861).

[6]Anderson, *op. cit.*, II, 698.

[7]Teel, *op. cit.*, II, 700.

gime, some of the north Mexican provinces were virtually independent—a golden opportunity for the Confederacy. In May, 1861, Secretary of State Robert Toombs had dispatched one John Pickett to Mexico as the minister of the Confederacy, and Pickett, upon arriving, had immediately set about stirring up an independence movement at Vera Cruz. A number of worried United States citizens in Mexico warned the State Department of the danger, whereupon Secretary of State William Seward threatened to occupy Sonora with Union troops. In spite of protests from Pickett, Juarez rammed a bill through the Mexican Congress authorizing Union soldiers to cross northern Mexico and use the port of Guaymas, both to mollify Seward and threaten Pickett with the prospect of a Mexican-United States alliance. Pickett was shortly recalled to Richmond.[8]

Though the central government of Mexico was thereafter hostile to the Confederacy, various state governors continued to toy with the ideas of independence or alliance with Richmond. Shortly after the Pickett incident the feudal governor of semi-autonomous Nueva Leon and Coahuila, Santiago Vidaurri, offered to annex his provinces to the South in return for a regiment of Texas troops and artillery, with which to win a revolution. Though Davis considered it "imprudent and impolitic" to accept Vidaurri's offer at the time, he instructed a Confederate spy in Monterey to send full particu-

---

[8]J. F. Rippy, "Mexican Projects of the Confederates, "*Southwestern Historical Quarterly,* XXII (1918), 291-293; *OR* I, L, pt. 1, 475, 831; Watford, *CHSQ,* 134; Watford, "Ambitions, "174. The Juarez bill was passed on June 20, 1861.

lars about the value of Vidaurri's states—for future reference.[9] Though the Confederacy's intention to annex Mexican territory with the consent of the Mexican government ended with Minister Pickett's recall, the South had not closed its eyes to its opportunities to steal northern Mexico state by state. Rather, this remained an argument for the invasion of New Mexico.

Another reason was the Southwest's abundance of recently discovered mineral wealth, including rich deposits of gold, which Lincoln considered essential to the successful prosecution of the war. At the time, it was commonly believed that if the rich mining regions of Arizona, Nevada and California had fallen into Confederate control, the disastrous inflation that marked the later decline of Confederate power would have been mitigated or abolished. Had the current of gold been diverted from Washington to Richmond, many held that the result would have been a proportionate reversal in the relative quotations of "Greenbacks" and "Graybacks." Some Confederates, including Baylor, considered the mineral wealth of Arizona to be its chief value.[10]

While Arizona offered gold and Mexico wheat and recruits, California (and possibly Baja California) would give the

[9]Watford, "Ambitions," 175. Davis still hoped to rectify Pickett's bungling, and get back in Juarez' good graces. He succeeded neither with Juarez nor Maximilian, though the latter favored the Confederacy as long as it kept the Union busy.

[10]Anderson, *op. cit.*, II, 697-698; *OR* I, IV, 23. Lincoln considered the flow of gold from the Southwest's mines to be the life-blood of the North's financial credit. Nevada, during the war, produced about fifty times the amount of specie that was in the Confederate treasury in 1865.

Confederacy a Pacific coastline over 1200 miles long. Northerners and Southerners alike admitted that this would break the blockade of rebel ports, since the United States Navy, in the early period of the war, was hardly capable of closing even the South's eastern ports. ". . . the ocean would have swarmed with *Alabamas*" from the three finest harbors on the Pacific coast, Guaymas, San Diego and San Francisco. In addition to the practical value of California, many feared or hoped that with its conquest the Confederacy would win a moral victory that the North could not reverse: "The conquest alone of this vast domain, in all probability, would have insured the recognition of the Confederacy by the European powers."[11]

Though the reasons for an invasion of New Mexico were substantial, what were its chances of success? A number of elements in the political, social and military condition of the Southwest gave the Confederates reason to be optimistic. In the first place, regardless of General Wright's precautions and temporary success in suppressing overt manifestations of secessionists in California, that State's rebel population was ready to fight a fierce guerrilla war in cooperation with an invading Confederate army. Whether such an operation would have been successful is debatable—California might not have seceded at all—but the probability remained that success was in favor of the rebels.[12]

---

[11]Anderson, *op. cit.,* II, 697. Wright agreed (*OR* I, L, pt. 1, 691). Note that the invasion was contemporary with the "Trent Affair."

[12]Anderson, *op. cit.,* II, 698. Caught between guerrillas on one side and rebels on the other, and outnumbered by each, it is doubtful that Wright could have won the state. Even one Confederate brigade would outnumber his command.

Similarly, the Mormon population of Utah, Arizona and California was held in submission to the Union only by the presence of army garrisons, and these people were generally expected to rebel at their first valid opportunity.[13] In fact, the entire Southwestern American population, drawn principally from the Southern states, was considered sympathetic to the Confederacy.[14]

Finally, the poor supplies and low morale of the Union military forces in the region suggested that they would be impotent against a concerted operation by a fresh Southern army. It was commonly asserted that the Confederates were responsible for the frequent and heavier raids by the Indian nations, and though documentary evidence is lacking to prove (or disprove) these claims the Indians did encourage the rebels by keeping the Nationals busy.[15]

Having heard and examined the arguments in favor of an invasion of New Mexico,

Mr. Jefferson Davis commissioned one H. H. Sibley . . . as a Brigadier General, and to raise three full regiments of cavalry in West Texas and proceed with all possible dispatch to meet these conditions and events as well as Californians, and to proceed forthwith without loss of time or failure to swipe the whole thing.[16]

---

[13]Watford, "Ambitions," *op. cit.,* 162; Anderson, *op. cit.,* II, 698. Though the Mormons bitterly opposed the occupation of Utah by Albert S. Johnston's army in 1857, their atrocities against "Gentiles," such as the Mountain Meadow Massacre, appeared to justify it.

[14]Watford, "Ambitions," 162; Waldrip, *op. cit.,* 166. Slavery was legal in New Mexico, but in 1860 only six slaves were there.

[15]Waldrip, *op. cit.,* 167.

[16]Noel, *op. cit.,* 56-57.

Henry H Sibley, BRIG. GEN. C.S.A.

The Confederate Invasion of New Mexico and Arizona

Except for the fact that Sibley was E. R. S. Canby's brother-in-law, Davis' appointee was the logical man to command the expedition. His long service in the Southwest and his office as commander of Fort Union had introduced him to the resources, government stores, terrain, and the condition and disposition of the enemy there. In August, with rather vague orders and with authorization to draw on Van Dorn's departmental stores for anything he needed, Sibley procured a new tunic with the three wreathed stars of a rebel brigadier sewn onto its buff collar and returned to Texas to begin preparations for the campaign.[17]

In New Mexico, meanwhile, Baylor had augumented the size of his battalion with three more companies of the 2d Texas (C, F and H) and with Arizona Volunteers, until his command numbered 922. Some of these men he sent to occupy abandoned posts like Fort Stanton, while others made sorties against Fort Craig. During the month of September four

---

[17]Teel, *op. cit.*, II, 700; Santee, *op. cit.*, 75; Samuel Cooper to Van Dorn, July 9, 1861, Sibley Jacket, National Archives; Sibley Jacket, National Archives, Confederate Archives, Chap. 1, File 86, p. 5 (Sibley's commission); *OR* I, IV, 93, 141. There is no record of the Sibley-Davis discussions, and, since Sibley's orders were verbal except for authorizations to establish civil government in Arizona, raise a brigade, and carry on a campaign as ordered by Davis (?), there is no proof Sibley was ordered to do more than win the Rio Grande. However, in a letter to Sibley of June 7, '62 (Rowland, *Jefferson Davis, Constitutionalist, His Letters, Papers, and Speeches,* [Jackson, Miss.: 1923], V, 271), Davis apologized for not supporting Sibley fully due to the war in the East (Peninsular Campaign), and praised him for all he had attempted and/or accomplished. In December, '61, Sibley told Capt. Teel (*op. cit.*, II, 700) that he was to conquer the whole Southwest. Whatever his orders he interpreted them as broadly as possible.

skirmishes were fought with Federal detachments, in most of which the Texans were victorious.[18]

Baylor's minor tactical successes did not blind him to his precarious position. In a letter to the Assistant Adjutant General of the Department of Texas, he explained:

I would respectfully ask, that if I am expected to hold fifteen hundred regular troops and four [two] regiments of New Mexican volunteers in check with less than four hundred men [in the immediate Mesilla area], that some other force be sent to operate against the Indians. I have already a detachment of twenty men at Camp Lancaster, Stockton and Fort Davis [guarding the communications to San Antonio]. I ordered Capt. [W. C.] Adams' company [C] to Davis, and ordered a detachment of fifteen men from Capt. Adams' company at Ft. Davis to make a camp at Eagle Springs, the point *where the Indians give much trouble.* I cannot at this time spare a man to garrison Fort Quitman [also on the San Antonio road.]
   . . . I have concentrated all the force I could muster about 7 miles above these head quarters [at Dona Ana, a small town above Mesilla], fearing an attack from Fort Craig, and am daily [expecting] a strong force from that point to move against me.[19]

By November, the threat from Craig and the rising enmity of the pro-Union Mexican peons of Dona Ana County obliged Baylor to withdraw his headquarters to Mesilla. Angered by this seeming act of cowardice, the secessionist editor of the *Mesilla Times* condemned the Governor in print. Baylor, judging that freedom of the press was abrogated by the virtual martial law he had imposed, shot the editor dead on

---

[18]Baylor to Capt. De le Smith, AAG, Dept. of Texas, Sept. 28, 1861, Baylor Papers, National Archives; *MR*, 2d Texas, Co. D., Sept.-Oct., 1861; Whitford, *op. cit.,* 29; Pettis, *op. cit.,* II, 104.

[19]Baylor to Capt. De le Smith, Sept. 28, 1861, *loc. cit.;* in this letter he also reported the largest skirmish in September with a contingent of Canby's cavalry, the so-called "Battle of Alamosa," Sept. 25-27, 1861.

Mesilla's main street. He surrendered himself to a military court, but was soon exonerated![20]

To regain the favor of the Americans in New Mexico Baylor dispatched contingents of his Arizona Volunteers to quiet the Indians around Dona Ana and to reopen the road to Tucson, blocked by warriors at Apache Pass. These expeditions had no permanent success.[21]

Rumors started drifting into Mesilla that a California brigade was marching via Guaymas across Sonora to the assistance of Col. Canby. Though untrue, they did indicate to Baylor that California was preparing to enter the war actively. While Baylor pondered this intelligence and considered a retreat into Texas, California continued to organize Col. Carleton's brigade for service in Arizona. On November 3d the first three volunteer companies of the brigade, under Col. Joseph R. West, arrived at Fort Yuma on the Colorado and started the initial preparations for the forthcoming campaign. By Nov. 26th, when Major Edwin Rigg replaced West, many wells had been dug in the desert toward Tucson and around Yuma, and a road for passing cannon had been surveyed from central California.[22]

---

[20]Baylor to H.Q., Dept. of Texas, Nov. 10, 1861, Baylor Jacket, National Archives; Smith, *op. cit.,* 91. This duel was not formal; Baylor happened to meet the editor on the street, where he ordered him to retract the article. When the editor refused, Baylor unholstered his pistol and fired. There is no evidence that the editor was armed.

[21]Smith, *op. cit.,* 91-96; Watford, *CHSQ.,* 130-131; Pettis, *op. cit.,* II, 104; Watford, "Ambitions," 166; *Mesilla Times,* Sept. 29, 1861. Capt. Thomas Helm's Arizona Volunteer company of miners was conspicuous in this operation.

Colonel Carleton, meanwhile, was actively engaged in procuring supplies for, and the organization and drill of, his 2,000 recruits. Since Arizona was barren, everything from beef herds to mustard, beans to charcoal, cartridges to cigars had to be collected beforehand. Almost all the manufactured items had to be shipped from the States by way of Panama or the Horn, and shipwreck, storms and administrative blunders vied with each other in delaying vital equipment. But nothing seemed to discourage Carleton, who, in that era before commanders enjoyed the luxury of trained staffs, was obliged to supervise everything from the procurement of pocket combs to drill-field discipline.[23]

With the Butterfield line cut off, Carleton knew nothing of the situation in New Mexico, though rumors were innumerable. To discover what was going on he sent spies to Tucson, who reported the town in turmoil and looking forward to the arrival of a Confederate army. One of his agents, in the late fall of 1861, finally sent positive word that "seven or eight hundred [!]" Texans had captured Fort Fillmore the previous July.[24]

---

[22]Watford, "Ambitions," 166; *OR* I, L, pt 1, pp. 137, 625, 661, 710-714, 742, 780, 808-811, 868-869; 932-933. Soon three other companies joined West's first three. This six-company garrison was composed of Companies A, B, C, E, G, and H of the First California Regiment, United States Volunteer Infantry.

[23]*OR* I, L, pt. 1, pp: 836-837, 773-780, 814, 819-820, 896, 943, 961, 975, 1033, 1049, 1052-1054, 987, 869, 822-823; Clendenen, *op. cit.,* 36. These enumerate Carleton's logistical, communications and transportation problems.

[24]*OR* I, L, pt. 1, 824-826, 854, 867. Without troops, Tucson became a haven for bandits and a favorite target for the Apache. Fred C. Buckner, one of Carleton's scouts, reported the people to be looking forward to the arrival of any troops, Union, Confederate or Mexican.

Almost simultaneously, Baylor's information about Carleton became more complete. In November, a group of California guerrillas slipped into Arizona and joined the Confederate army, bringing news that no Federals were marching across Sonora, but that some were concentrating at Fort Yuma. Baylor reported this to General Paul O. Hebert, who had since replaced Van Dorn as commander of the Department of Texas, and went on to suggest that a body of soldiers be sent to western Arizona to observe Carleton and contact California secessionists. As a precaution, he also asked Simeon Hart of El Paso to collect all the available wagons in the area in case the Confederates were obliged to retreat to central Texas.[25]

Evidently Baylor was still unaware that assistance was on the way. In San Antonio, Gen. Sibley mustered the first company of his brigade on August 27, and by November 15 thirty full companies were enrolled. It seems that "the Sibley Brigade California deal" was considered a choice assignment by most military-age gentlemen of the region, and obtaining recruits proved rather easy.[26] The companies were organized into three regiments, the 4th (Col. James Reily, Lt. Col. W. R. Scurry, Maj. Henry Ragnet), 5th (Col. Thomas Green, Lt. Col. Henry McNeill, Maj. Sam Lockridge) and 7th Texas Mounted Volunteers (Col. William Steele, Lt. Col. J. S. Sutton, Maj. A. P. Bagby). The officers, many of whom were old

---

[25]C. Evans, *op. cit.*, XI, 49; *OR* I, L, pt. 1, 716. A smallpox epidemic ravaged Baylor's command about this time.

[26]Noel, *op. cit.*, 57.

campaigners or leading Texas politicans, were to prove exceptionally good commanders: Scurry, Green and Steele subsequently rose to command brigades, while, in the closing days of the war, Bagby became a Major-General. Sibley's adjutant, A. M. Jackson, was one of the most able administrators in Texas, and an aide-de-camp, Tom Ochiltree, later became governor of the Lone Star State.[27]

The common troopers of the Texas Brigade were typical of Texans in the Confederate army; they were

... three thousand five hundred [including Baylor's battalion] of ... the best that ever threw leg over a horse or that had ever sworn allegiance to any cause. All-around men, natural born soldiers, they were under twenty-five, with a liberal sprinkling of older men who had seen more or less service on the frontier.[28]

Rough and ready plainsmen toughened by long experience with desert weather and hostile Indians, they were fierce in battle, but their determination not to submit to army discipline was just as fierce. They swore allegiance to the Confederacy and would keep faith as long as the Confederacy did not try to curb their allegiance to Texas or their ideal of personal liberty. Some were dedicated secessionists, like Private Joseph Sayers, who followed Ochiltree to the Texas governor's chair. Others had no cause but loot.[29]

---

[27]*MR*, 4, 5, 7 Texas cavalry, National Archives; Twitchell, *OSF* III, 38. Brief biographies appear in C. Evans, *op. cit.*, XI; biographies and/or photos in F. T. Miller, *The Photographic History of the Civil War* (New York: 1911), X. At least one junior officer, Capt. William Hardeman, commanding Company A, 4th Texas, later became a Brigadier. His brother, Peter, commanded Company A of Baylor's battalion.

[28]Noel, *op. cit.* 57.

[29]Whitford, *op. cit.*, p. 74, 126. Sayers was soon commissioned Lieutenant on the staff of the 5th Texas.

The lack of supplies for the recruits in San Antonio did not help the officers impose discipline. ". . . they do just as they please, and you know what men off on a long trip please to do . . ."[30] The paymaster seldom appeared, and when he did the crude Confederate paper he distributed proved to be almost worthless, since the majority of the local citizens, simple Mexicans, refused to accept it. In this particularly individualistic brigade discipline could only have been imposed by a commander particularly blessed with the leadership qualities that inspire men to follow without question, but Sibley's one vice prevented him from being fully trusted by his troops. "The Commanding General," wrote one, ". . . was an old army officer whose love for liquor exceeded that for home, country or God."[31] Even this attitude degenerated after the battle of Val Verde indicated that Sibley's taste for whiskey was married to personal cowardice.

Sibley could only train his undisciplinable troopers as dragoons (mounted infantry), rather than as heavy cavalry. During the training period at San Antonio he worked industriously to collect ordnance from every available source, and made arrangements with the ubiquitous Simeon Hart to have provisions and money collected for his army in El Paso. While Sibley was working, his men speculated between drills about

---

[30]*OR* I, L, pt. 1, 1012. The shortage of provisions was to plague the brigade throughout the campaign. Coffee and pork products (staples, on the books) were unavailable. The troops supplied their own weapons: shotguns, muskets, Colts, Bowie knives and lassos. Regarding Texans' discipline, Gen. John B. Hood's Texas Brigade was known as the wildest unit in Robert E. Lee's Army.

[31]MR 7th Texas, Co. I (Dec. 31, 1861); *OR* IV, I, 89; Noel, *op. cit.,* 62.

the brigade's objective; some argued for Virginia, others Mexico, and others Missouri and Arkansas. Some were relieved and others were surprised when Lt. Joseph Sayers rode through camp one day shouting orders for a westward march.[32]

The 4th and 5th Texas left San Antonio between October 22d and November 2d, and by November 8th the point of Col. Reily's column was 250 miles west along the road to El Paso. On the 18th Sibley packed his headquarters equipment and, with Steele's regiment, followed the rest of the brigade.[33]

At least one colonel was dissatisfied with the developing campaign. On the 19th Reily wrote one M. D. Miller that "I am pushing on with all possible speed to El Passo [*sic*] to support Baylor—But my dear friend I do not believe there is to be much if any fighting in New Mexico. My [*sic*] regiment is too fine a one to be wasted in forts & inactivity."[34]

While the brigade moved over the west Texas desert, scouts observed Indian signs indicating that the Comanche-Apache nations were massing to attack the Confederates. Warned of the danger, Sibley, whose "friendship with the

---

[32]Harris, *op. cit.*, 22, 26; OR I, IV, 134-135; 141-143; Noel, *op. cit.*, 65; Robert Seay,"Incidents of Glorieta Battle . . ." *Sante Fe New Mexican*, Aug. 13, 1906; Howland, *loc. cit.*, Aug. 7; Harris and the rest also mention Utah and even more distant objectives.

Merchant Hart contracted with Sibley to have on hand, when Sibley arrived at Fort Bliss, El Paso, in December, 40,000 or 50,000 pounds of flour and an additional $40,000 or $50,000 for the purchase of flour, beans, salt, beef, corn and soap.

[33]Watford, "Ambitions," 170; OR I, IV, 151. Co. K, 7th Texas, remained in garrison at San Antonio.

[34]Letter, Reily to Miller, Nov. 19 '61, Reily Jacket, National Arch.

Indians was very great, while that of his brother-in-law, Canby, . . . was nil," thereafter took care to leave peace signs along his trail. In this way the threat of a "round-robin" war, with Indians, Federals and Confederates all shooting at one another, was temporarily nullified.[35]

The rear of Sibley's column reached El Paso and went into quarters at Fort Bliss in mid-December. On the 14th the General assumed formal command of all Confederate forces on the Rio Grande above Fort Quitman, and on the 20th issued a proclamation to the people of Arizona promising that the Confederate government would protect their civil liberties, abolishing Union taxes, and inviting officers and men of the Union army to join the Confederates. Baylor's government was recognized and, though Baylor lost command of the troops in the Territory, he retained the office of governor with the new brevet rank of Colonel. This division of authority left Baylor supreme in civil affairs and Sibley in military, a situation which was almost sure to create friction.[36]

In a discussion with Captain Teel, Sibley confirmed that "on to San Francisco would be the watchword . . .," and expressed his intention to incorporate the North Mexican states into the Confederacy through a process of military occupation with the consent of the provincial governors.[37] On December 26th

[35]Harris, *op. cit.*, 26; Noel, *op. cit.*, 58-59. Noel was one of the three scouts who first reported finding the Concho (*i.e.*, Apache, Gila, Comanche and Pawnee) Indian signs. He estimated that every tribe and clan within 1,200 miles knew of Sibley's advance.

[36]*OR* I, IV, 89-90, 157-158, 158-159; Sibley's Proclamation, Dec. 20, 1861, Sibley Jacket, National Archives; Special Order No. 105, Dec. 15, 1861, Baylor Jacket, National Archives; Teel, *op. cit.*, 700.

[37]Teel, *op. cit.*, 700.

General Sibley Wins a Command

Col. Reily was detached from line service (Lt. Col. Scurry took command of the 4th) and was ordered to proceed to Chihuahua and Sonora to enlist their aid in the cause of the Confederacy. Governor Terrazas of Chihuahua formally and graciously received the uniformed ambassador in January, and Reily soon reported that Terrazas had agreed to refuse passage across his province to Union troops and to supply Sibley generously.[38] While in Chihuahua Reily wrote Confederate Postmaster-General John Reagan that this "rich and glorious neighbor" would ". . . improve by being under the Confederate flag . . . We must have Sonora and Chihuahua. . . With [them] we gain Southern California . . ."[39]

Sibley's high opinion of Reily's success was dashed when he received a note from Terrazas "clarifying" Chihuahua's position: the Governor was still willing to supply Sibley (for hard cash) and to store materiel for him south of the Rio Grande, but he refused Sibley permission to chase Indians into Mexican territory and said that if orders came from Mexico City, he would be obliged to let Federal troops march through his state. Terrazas probably waited for Reily to leave his capital before "diplomatically" throwing cold water on the young man's enthusiasm; the Governor was between

---

[38]Special Order No. 111, Dec. 26, 1861, Reily Jacket, National Archives; OR I, IV, 167-168, 170-171; OR I, IX, 174. Reily was received at the Governor's palace formally, while wearing the gold-trimmed, triple starred gray uniform of a colonel of cavalry, C. S. A. He considered this recognition of his uniform as that of a sovereign nation to be the first "recognition" of the Confederate States Government by a "foreign power."

[39]OR I, L, pt. 1, 825-826, dated Jan. 20, by which time Reily had already left Chihuahua's capital.

three fires, the Union, the Confederacy and Mexico, and he was not willing to add fuel to one if he was to be burned in return by the others.[40]

Meanwhile, on January 11th, Sibley had moved his brigade from El Paso to Mesilla, where it shared the scanty supplies, the little, richly-engraved, worthless money, and epidemics of smallpox and pneumonia, with Baylor's battalion. Altogether, Sibley had thirty-six companies of Texas dragoons, half a dozen of Arizona Volunteer cavalry, one of Arizona infantry, one Texas battery and three regimental artillery sections (one or two guns each) with which to conquer the Southwest. Since the regimental records had been left at El Paso, and since from this time forward there was no direct communication with Richmond and hardly any to or from San Antonio, Sibley's 3,700 men, about to embark on one of the most ambitious campaigns of the war, were isolated from the nation they hoped to double in size.[41]

Therefore Sibley did not learn until he returned from New Mexico in the spring of 1862 that on January 18th the Confederate Congress had passed legislation providing for the civil organization of the Arizona Territory. This bill, patterned after the Northwest Ordinance of 1787, declared that

---

[40]*OR* I, IX, 171-172, Terrazas to Sibley, Jan. 11, 1862.

[41]*MR* 2d Texas, Co. E, & 5th Texas, Cos. G & I (Oct.-Apr., 1862); *Official Reports of Battles, Published by the Congress of the Confederate States* (New York: 1863) (cited: *ORCSA,* p. xix), 177 (Sibley's general report, May 4th, 1862). All of Sibley's cannon were battalioned under general command of Capt. Trevanion T. Teel, Baylor's chief of artillery. The cannon, about twelve in number, were all light howitzers mounted on "mountain (exceptionally light) carriages."

the "Confederate Territory of Arizona" was bounded by Texas, Mexico, the Colorado River and the 34th parallel, and was to be governed by an appointed governor and an elected bicameral legislature. All acts of the legislature were to be subject to review by the Confederate Congress, but the Territory was granted the authority to appoint a Congressional Delegate. The capital was reestablished at Mesilla and slavery, of course, was legalized. President Davis declared the law in effect by a proclamation published on February 14th, and in a subsequent executive appointment confirmed Baylor as the Territorial Governor. In March, the United States Congress, which naturally did not recognize the "rebel" legislature's act, introduced a similar Arizona Territorial bill which differed from the Southern legislation only in the matters of slavery and boundary lines (the North's boundaries were a closer approximation of those of the present states of Arizona and New Mexico). However, a year passed before this bill became law.[42]

Unaware of the war being carried on with legislative acts along the Richmond-Washington front, Sibley continued his war of bullets in New Mexico. Having established a military hospital in the town of Dona Ana, Sibley started his brigade toward Santa Fe during the first week of February, 1862. He chose to march up the Rio Grande for a number of reasons: the land irrigated by it was the only land in the Territory on

---

[42]Donnell, *op. cit.*, 158; R. L. Rodgers, "The Confederate States Organized Arizona in 1862," *Southern Historical Society Papers*, XXVIII, (1900), 224; *OR* IV, I, 930; *OR* I, L, pt. 1, 925; Wyllys, *op. cit.*, 35.

which his army could live by forage; there were rich quarter-master's stores at Fort Craig, Albuquerque and Santa Fe; and $275,000 in cash was reported to be at Fort Union. Finally, by gaining control of the western terminus of the Santa Fe Trail, he would further isolate the semi-rebellious popula-tions of Colorado, Utah, Nevada and California from the far-off Washington government.[43]

Abandoned Fort Thorn was quickly won, and from there on the 7th of February he set out toward Fort Craig with about 2,600 men—the 4th and 5th Texas, most of Baylor's battalion under Major Charles Pyron, Sutton's battalion of the 7th, some Arizona Volunteers and the entire artillery battalion.[44] The march over the wastelands of the Jornado del Muerto was made worse by always-threatening Indians, whom "we dread . . . worse than the Lincolnites, by odds,"[45] and by a freak spell of bitterly cold, snowy weather. But by February 12th the Confederate troops successfully dragged their long artillery and wagon train to a point only seven miles south of Fort Craig.[46]

At Craig, Canby had been aware that the rebels were in Mesilla since January, and had redoubled his efforts to ready his garrison for battle. The supply and money problem had

[43]*ORCSA*, 177; Twitchell, *OSF* III, 24; Harris, *op. cit.,* 28.

[44]Watford, *CHSQ*, 132; Evans, *op. cit.,* XI, 258. Many convalescents, most of the Arizona Volunteers, and over half of Steele's 7th Texas were left behind to garrison Mesilla, El Paso, Dona Ana, Fort Stanton, and the surrounding areas.

[45]*Texas State Gazette* (Austin), Feb. 15, 1862.

[46]E. Hanna, Journal, Texas State Library, Austin, p. 2; Santee, *op. cit.,* 69; Harris, *op. cit.,* 29.

become so acute that two mutinies had to be put down, for rations were—and would continue to be—perpetually short. Navajo Indians had attacked a few of his scouting parties and, if all this were not enough to destroy the morale of his troops, some men and a fair number of officers had deserted.[47]

But all was not hopeless. A staunch company of independent Colorado Volunteers, under Captain William Dodd, had unexpectedly arrived, and a few more companies of third-rate New Mexicans had been raised by Col. Roberts. By February, Canby's vigorous propagandizing so transformed the morale of his 3,810 soldiers that they manifested a "very good spirit!"[48]

A rebel reconnaissance in force against Craig's outer works on the afternoon of February 16th was turned back, convincing General Sibley that it would be futile to assault the fort, "and that our only hope of success was to force the enemy to an open field fight." Later the same day illness confined him to an ambulance, and Colonel Green of the 5th regiment assumed direction of the brigade. A typical New Mexico dust storm paralyzed all operations on the 17th and 18th, but on the 19th Green started moving the army.[49]

Though Craig, situated on the west bank of the Rio Grande and controlling the road from Mesilla to Albuquerque, could not be assaulted directly, it could be outflanked and its com-

---

[47]OR I, IV, 82, 87; *Conduct of the War*, III, 366, 370, 371; *MR* 1st N. M., Co. I (Nov.-Dec., 1861), 2d N. M., Co. E (Jan. 26, 1862).

[48]Twitchell, *OSF* III, 18; Roe, *loc. cit.*, Nov. 3, 1910; Waldrip, *op. cit.*, 176.

[49]Pettis, *op. cit.*, II, 104; ORCSA, 178; Waldrip, *op. cit.*, 177; *et. al.*

ON THE MARCH

munications with Santa Fe cut. Green reasoned that if he passed to the east bank of the river, marched northward under cover of a range of hills running parallel with the water and terminating at the Mesa de la Contedera, seven miles above the fort, and then re-forded the river at Val Verde, he would place his army between Canby's and the North. The hills on the east bank would also offer excellent artillery positions from which to bombard Fort Craig.[50]

By the 20th the Confederate army, under cover of the hills between it and the river, was opposite Fort Craig. Green attempted to place artillery on the heights overlooking the river and fort, but Canby had anticipated the move and the Confederates found the position strongly held by New Mexican infantry under Colonels Pino and Robert Stapleton, and cavalry under Capt. James C ydon. Pino's position, between Green and the river, forced the Texans to make a "dry camp" on the night of the 20th.[51]

About midnight, Captain Graydon tried to blow up a few rebel picket posts by sending mules loaded with barrels of fused gunpowder into the Confederate lines, but the faithful old army mules insisted on wandering back toward the Union camp before blowing to bits. Although the only casualties

---

[50]Watford, "Ambitions," 171. Sketch-map No. 1, on the "Battle of Valverde" map, *post.* p. 74, indicates the terrain and strategy. Green could not pass up the road on the west bank because it traversed open country and was controlled by the artillery in Fort Craig. Had such a maneuver been attempted, the Confederates would have exposed their right flank to sorties directed against it from the fort.

[51]*ORCSA*, 178; Harris, *op. cit.*, 31; Pettis, *op. cit.*, II, 107, 104-105; Watford, "Ambitions," 171.

were two mules,[52] the explosions stampeded a herd of Confederate beef cattle into the Unions lines, so depriving Green's troops of some much-needed provisions.[53]

Sibley resumed command of the army shortly after dawn and sent Maj. Pyron's battalion ahead to secure the river ford at Val Verde. The Confederates were unaware that Canby had ordered Col. Roberts to take all the Union cavalry, Capt. David Brotherton's and Capt. Charles Ingraham's companies of Regular infantry, two companies of New Mexican infantry (Mortimer's and Hubbell's), Dodd's Colorado Volunteers, Capt. Alexander McRae's Provisional Battery (two sections), and Lt. Robert Hall's two twenty-four pounder howitzers to the ford to hold it for the Union army. Both commands reached Val Verde at about 8:00 a.m.; after a short small-arms duel between infantry and cavalry, each aligned on opposite banks of the river and continued the fire-fight. The Federals on the west bank were the first to receive the support of artillery, though at about 9:00 a.m. Lt. John Reily's two gun section of Confederate artillery arrived and unlimbered. With it came Ragnet's battalion of the 4th Texas and, a few moments later, the entire regiment.[54]

---

[52]Pettis, *op. cit.*, II, 105n; Harris, *op. cit.*, 31; *Conduct of the War*, III, 367.

[53]*Conduct of the War*, III, 367. Following the Battle of Val Verde the Confederates found themselves cut off from Dona Ana with but five days' rations on hand.

[54]*ORCSA*, 178, 190, 202, 196, 199, 191; Joseph Bell, "Val Verde" (ed. by M. L. Crimmins), *NMHR* VII (1932) (cited: Crimmins, "VV"), 348; Pettis *op. cit.*, II, 106; *MR* 5th N.M., H.Q. (Feb. 28, 1862); Twitchell, *OSF*, III, 27. Col. Roberts rushed forward with 220 cavalry early on the 21st and opened the contest with Pyron, whose men were rushing out of order to reach

General Sibley Wins a Command

With the brassy ring of howitzers mingling with the rattle of musketry and echoing over the fields to the accompaniment of clanking sabres and shouts of war, the Battle of Val Verde had begun.

---

the water, on the east bank. Pyron forced him across the ford to the west bank where, with the help of reinforcements, Roberts stabilized his front with his cannon at the flanks. By 9:00 a.m. Pyron had arranged his command along the river with Lt. Reily's (Col. Reily's younger brother) section on the right and Scurry's regiment (with Ragnet's battalion on the left) and Pyron's battalion extending southward. The Confederate right was covered by a copse of trees and the left by the Mesa de la Contedera, while Roberts was on generally open ground.

Thomas Green
COLONEL, 5 TEXAS

Confederate Regimental
Commanders

John R Baylor
LT. COL.   2 TEXAS

William Steele
COLONEL, 7 TEXAS

William R. Scurry
LT. COL.,   4 TEXAS

CHAPTER III

CAPTAIN HUNTER CONQUERS A DESERT

THOUGH Col. Roberts' heavier cannon were able to silence Lt. Reily's small section in short order, the battle remained a tactical stalemate until noon. Then Canby, who had left a skeleton garrison at Craig, arrived to take personal charge, bringing with him Capt. Richard Selden's battalion of Regulars and Pino's and Carson's New Mexican regiments. Swiftly Canby ordered Maj. Thomas Duncan's Regular cavalry and Selden's infantry to cross the river and assault the Confederate line. When they shortly succeeded in driving the Confederates a mile from the river, Canby started crossing the rest of his army and forming a line of battle on the east bank, with the artillery on the flanks.

The initial impetus of the Union charge petered out against a wall of metal thrown from Teel's rebel batteries, which had just arrived on the field. In short order Lockridge's battalion and then the entire 5th Texas came up with orders from Sibley to reinforce the wavering rebel front. After some slight shifting of commands, a stable line was drawn: Scurry's 4th held the right, supported by Pyron, while on the 4th's left

Lockridge, Green's 5th, and Ragnet's battalion extended the front toward the Mesa. Teel's guns, alone or in sections, were brought into action wherever they were needed.

About 1:30 Sibley again relinquished command to Col. Green, claiming that he was "completely exhausted."[1] At least one Johnny Reb was convinced that his brand of exhaustion came bottled in bond, and that he was "so much under the influence of liquor" that he could no longer direct the battle.[2] For the rest of the campaign Sibley's influence steadily waned; "He was utterly incompatible (some say a coward) . . . At any rate after [Val Verde] we never saw him again."[3]

Green ordered Sutton's battalion of the 7th, which had been guarding the wagons in the rear, to come into line between the 5th Texas and Ragnet's battalion of the 4th. This cost the army 100 wagons "containing the entire kits, blankets, books and papers of this regiment [the 4th]"[4] for as soon as Sutton left a nicely timed raid by Stapleton and Graydon spirited them away.

Canby, meanwhile was making the final arrangements in his line. On the north was McRae's battery, supported by Dodd, Carson and Selden; near the ford was Capt. Robert Lord's battalion of Regular cavalry; and over a mile to the

---

[1] *ORCSA*, 179.

[2] R. E. Twitchell, *The Leading Facts of New Mexican History* (Cedar Rapids: 1912), II, 377. The rebel soldier is unidentified.

[3] Letter, H. C. Wright to Tom Greer, Sept. 27, 1927; *MS* in the Museum of New Mexico Library Vertical File, Santa Fe (cited: Wright, Letter).

[4] *ORCSA*, 179.

south was Hall's artillery section, supported by Duncan's cavalry. The mile gap in the center was supposed to be filled by Pino, but his regiment chose this most inopportune moment to mutiny, and scattered in all directions. This was the turning point in the Battle of Val Verde.

After an artillery barrage, Canby sent Dodd's Colorado company against the exposed right flank of Scurry's exhausted regiment, but without a moment to spare, Capt. Willis Lang's *elite* company B of the 5th Texas, armed with sabres and guidon-bedecked lances, charged the Colorado Company and forced it to fall back. But Dodd's men, formed in a hollow square, behaved like Regulars in the face of the cavalry charge, nearly annihilating Lang's command.

The initiative had shifted to the rebels. Green threw Ragnet's battalion against Hall's battery which Canby saved by drawing Carson's regiment from McRae's battery supports and sending it to the far right. This was exactly what Green wanted, for now, in two successive charges by Lockridge, Pyron, Scurry and his own 5th, he fell on the weakened Union left, killed McRae, took his battery, routed Carson's volunteers, and won the field. Teel brought his guns to the newly won position, added McRae's abandoned pieces to his own, and aided by Scurry's infantry, blew squads and platoons of fleeing Federals out of the water, and sent the rest scurrying to Craig.[5]

---

[5]The best secondary account of the battle appears in Twitchell, *OSF*, III; Confederate reports appear in the *ORCSA*, while reports by officers of both sides appear in *OR* I, IX. The following primary accounts are valuable: Pettis,

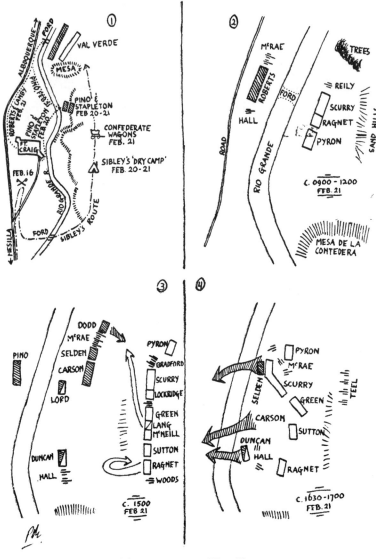

THE BATTLE OF VAL VERDE

Captain Hunter Conquers a Desert

Sibley resumed command of the Confederates at 7:00 p.m., pulled elements of Scurry's regiment which had crossed the river back to the east bank, and breveted Scurry on the spot to the rank of Colonel for "gallant and meritorious conduct."[6] Canby, meanwhile, herded his demoralized Regulars and Colorado Volunteers back to Craig, and even succeeded in persuading one company of Pino's mutinous regiment, Capt. José D. Sena's, to return to the colors. While these men put the fort in shape for an expected siege, the Union officers counted heads and discovered that 306 officers and men were casualties or missing. This total did not include "missing" New Mexicans, but Canby frankly reported that their loss "adds to rather than diminishes our strength."[7]

The Confederate losses had been much lighter, for there were but 185 casualties, and only one man was missing! Dur-

op. cit., II; Crimmins, "VV;" Lt. Col. A. W. Evans, "Canby at Val Verde," B&L II; Anderson, op. cit., II; Roe, loc. cit., Nov. 3, 1910; Conduct of the War, III; Whitford, op. cit. (especially good in reference to Dodd's company); Howland, loc. cit., Aug. 7, 1906. My account is drawn chiefly from Twitchell and the ORCSA.

It is with regret that space limitations prevent me from going into more detail regarding Val Verde. Like Cowpens in the Revolution, it was a gem of a little battle (from the Confederate standpoint), illustrating the American soldier's genius for small, tactical engagements. Green had never before held an independent command, and yet he handled his 2,600 men with the finesse of a professional. The only major Confederate blunder, the loss of the "dry camp" and wagons, can be blamed on his inexperience more than anything else. Canby's plans were equally good but, except for the Regulars and Dodd's company, he was saddled with far inferior troops.

[6]ORCSA, 201; Harris, op. cit., 38; Special Order, unnumbered, Feb. 21, 1862, Scurry Jacket, National Archives.

[7]Twitchell, OSF III, 33; Crimmins, "VV," 352; Pettis, op. cit., II, 108; OR I, IX 487.

ing the night a truce was arranged for both sides to collect their dead and wounded, but, under cover of the white flags, some enterprising Federals managed to salvage many small arms, two cannon, and other abandoned equipment, which they carried to Craig in the dead wagons.[8]

Canby buried his dead with full honors at Craig the next morning, while the Confederates collected theirs in an unmarked trench in the bloody soil of Val Verde. Later that day a delegation of three rebel officers rode into Craig, both to observe its condition and demand its surrender, but they were unceremoniously ushered out by Canby. On the basis of their observations, Sibley decided not to besiege the fort. His decision might have been different had he known that many of the "cannon" his delegation saw on the fort's walls were "Quaker guns," that is, painted logs.[9]

Owing to the loss and destruction of animals and wagons during the battle, Sibley had only five days' rations on hand. Canby's garrison blocked his supply line to Mesilla and, since he had not the provisions to mount a siege and since it seemed a grave political error to retreat to Dona Ana, Sibley decided in a council of war to continue the march to Albuquerque.[10]

---

[8]*ORCSA*, 195, 179. The Federals also managed to carry off a rebel company guidon and a regimental battle-flag which had been left on the field. Sibley protested to Canby about this unchivalrous method of collecting battle trophies,

[9]Twitchell, *OSF*, III, 36, 38; Harris, *op. cit.*, 39; Whitford, *op. cit.*, 68. The three officers were Col. Scurry, Capt. D. Shannon, and Lt. Ochiltree.

[10]*ORCSA*, 180. Sibley intended to forage during the march. Because of the shortage of horses occasioned by the fight, he dismounted the 4th Texas. "I now feel the pleasure of soldiering in New Mexico more plainly," wrote disgruntled Pvt. Hanna in his Journal, p. 7.

Captain Hunter Conquers a Desert

The Confederates broke camp on the 24th and started up the rich Rio Grande Valley. They left Canby, bottled up in Craig, in the midst of a bitter verbal war about his capabilities as a commander. It was not until after his death at the hands of Modoc Jack in 1873 that many of his officers became reconciled to the fact that he was not to blame for the tactical disaster on the 21st of February, 1862.[11]

Meanwhile, far to the west of both Sibley and Canby, another phase of the Conquest of the Southwest opened on the 28th of February, when Captain Sherod Hunter's 100-man company of Confederate Arizona Volunteers swung down the dusty street of isolated, lawless Tucson. Shortly after Sibley had left Dona Ana, Governor Baylor had ordered Hunter to take formal possession of western Arizona for the Confederacy, to secure its mineral resources and its citizens' allegiance, and to bring the Confederate flag to the frontier of California. When Hunter arrived at Tucson the people, sick of raids by desperados, Mexican bandits and Apaches, received his men cordially and without incident, though they failed to display any particular devotion to the strange banner that the rebels carried.[12]

On their part, Hunter's men were careful not to stir up any latent enmity toward themselves, and occupied themselves by foraging for grain and provisions. On the 29th Col. Reily

---

[11]*ORCSA*, 180; Pettis, *op. cit.*, II, 108; A. Evans, *op. cit.*, 700. Even achievements like *Maj. Gen.* Canby's negotiations for the surrender of 80,000 rebels in the Gulf States (including every rebel in the Trans-Mississippi Dept.) in 1865 failed to change some minds.

[12]C. Evans, *op. cit.*, XI, 293; *OR* I, IX, 868, 707; Wyllys, *op. cit.*, 35.

and his bodyguard, traveling from Chihuahua to Sonora, happened to arrive in town and, at Hunter's invitation, Reily gave a speech and participated in a formal flag-raising ceremony in the town plaza. The ceremony was hardly over before Hunter had his men fanning out over the countryside, confiscating mines owned by Northerners and making sorties against the ever-troublesome Apache.[13]

One of his detachments discovered an abundance of military stores and provisions at the nearby Pima Indian Villages. The Indians confirmed rumors Hunter had heard in Tucson stating that agents from Fort Yuma were in the area preparing the way for the advance of a Union brigade from California. To learn more, Hunter ordered elements of his command to ride toward the Colorado River, and by mid-April rebel dragoons were less than fifty miles from California.[14]

On the far side of the Colorado, Col. Carleton had learned from spies and the Yuma Indians that Hunter's men were near Tucson. Toward the end of February he sent Capt. William McCleave and a squad of cavalry on a reconnaissance mission into Arizona in order to confirm his intelligence and to contact one Ami White, a Tucson miller who was stocking sup-

---

[13]Wyllys, *op. cit.*, 35; *OR* I, L, pt. 1, 944-945; *OR* I, IX, 707. There is no evidence to show that Hunter could afford either the time or the men necessary to get the mines producing for the Confederacy.

The reader will remember that Col. Reily had completed a diplomatic mission to Chihuahua and was scheduled to make a similar attempt in neighboring Sonora. His bodyguard consisted of twenty cavalrymen and two subalterns.

[14]*OR* I, L, pt. 1, 137, 139, 810; *OR* I, IX, 597. It is probable that Hunter knew something of Carleton's activities before he left Mesilla, since Baylor had received intelligence regarding Carleton's recruiting activities in November, 1861, before Hunter left.

plies for Carleton at his own mill and in the Pima villages. When, in mid-March, McCleave approached White's house, he was unaware that the miller had been arrested and that Hunter was using the building as his headquarters. The man who answered McCleave's knock greeted the Union officer with cocked revolvers in his hands and the words, "I am Captain Hunter of the Southern army . . . If you make a single motion, I'll blow your brains out." Faced with that rather nasty alternative, McCleave surrendered—only to add to Hunter's apprehensions about an "invasion" from California.[15]

While Hunter probed westward, Col. Reily left Arizona for the capital of Sonora and the palace of Governor Don Ignacio Pesqueira. Here he was received as graciously as he had been in Chihuahua, and negotiated with the Governor for a number of concessions: that Sonora forbid the use of Guaymas to the United States; that it refuse the Union army transit across its territory; that it grant free entry and passage to the Southern army; and that it supply the Confederates with food and military stores. The Governor verbally assured Reily that not only would Sonora agree to these provisions, but that the province would rebel from the Republic if the Juarez government questioned its authority to do so.[16]

---

[15]Sacramento *Union*, May 23, 1862; *OR* I, L, pt. 1, 137. McCleave was sent to Dona Ana County and imprisoned by Col. Steele until he was exchanged four months after his capture; the nine men of his squad were paroled by Hunter.

[16]*OR* I, IX, 707; *OR* I, L, pt. 1, 1032-1033, 989, 1013, 1042; Donnell, *op. cit.*, 160. Noel's suggestion (*op. cit.*, 60) that Reily's immediate objective was annexation of Sonora is not substantiated, though very possibly it was Sibley's long-range plan. Incidentally, Reily received the same formal recognition in

The Confederate Invasion of New Mexico and Arizona

Unfortunately for Reily, W. G. Moody, an enterprising reporter for the *San Francisco Bulletin,* managed to steal copies of Reily's letter of introduction from Sibley and some of his notes, and transmitted them to General Wright in California. Within a matter of days Wright had a gunboat standing off the harbor at Guaymas and a letter prepared for Pesqueira, one of the most diplomatic threats ever penned. Wright started by congratulating Pesqueria for refusing (!) Reily's propositions, and then went on to assure him that "under no circumstances will the Government of the United States permit the rebel hordes to take refuge in Sonora. I have an army of ten [*i.e.,* four or five] thousand men ready to pass the frontier and protect your government and your people."[17] Upon receiving Wright's letter Pesqueira, like the Governor of Chihuahua, decided to reconsider, and sent a letter to Sibley stating that Reily's claims of success had been "exaggerated, or perhaps badly interpreted."[18] By August, when the Sibley brigade had been chased out of Arizona, Pesqueira was definitely on the winning side, for he dispatched a letter to Wright promising that if any "rebels" (now he used the word!) set foot on Mexican soil, he would exterminate them.[19]

Sonora that he had in Chihuahua; one's interpetation of whether the Confederacy was in fact recognized as a legitimate government depends on whether one believes sovereign states in a federal government without much power (as the Juarez government) can act independently in recognizing a foreign power.

[17]*OR* I, L, pt. 1, 1047-1048, May 1st, 1862. Moody stole the letters from the office of Pesqueira's translator, when the latter left to take Spanish copies to the Governor.

[18]*OR* I, L, pt. 1, 1117-1118, June 2, 1862.

[19]*OR* I, L, pt. 2, 93, August 29, 1862.

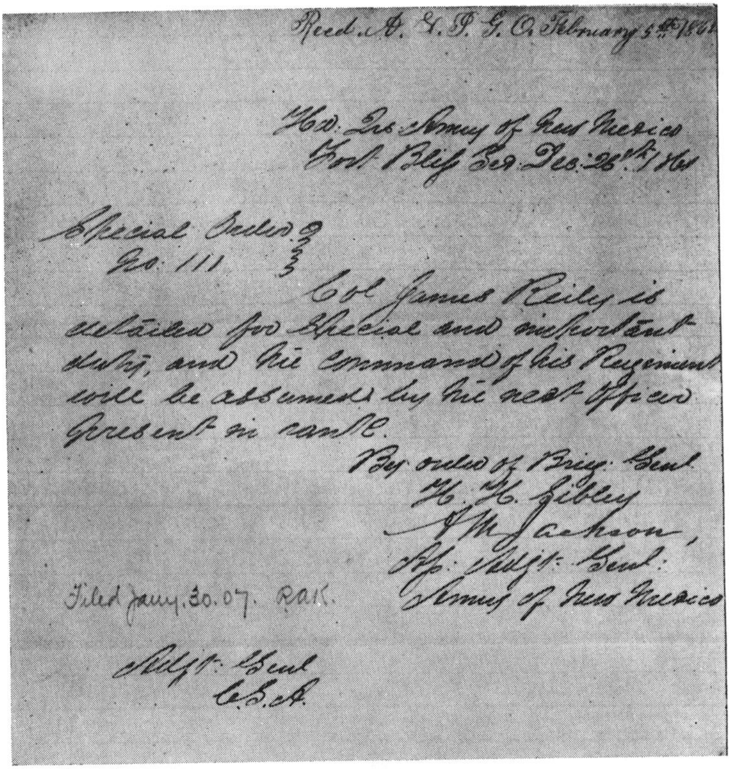

Recd. A. & I. G. O. February 5th 1862

Hd. Qrs. Army of New Mexico
Fort Bliss Tex. Dec. 26th 1861

Special Orders }
No. 111 }

Col James Reily is detailed for special and important duty, and the command of his Regiment will be assumed by the next Officer present in camp.

By order of Brig. Genl
H. H. Sibley
T M Jackson,
Asst. Adjt. Genl.
Army of New Mexico

Filed Jany. 30. 07. RAK.

Adjt. Genl
C.S.A.

COL. JAMES REILY BECOMES A DIPLOMAT

PIGEON'S RANCH

Captain Hunter Conquers a Desert

Somehow Sibley missed an opportunity to send a representative to Santiago Vidaurri, Governor of Coahuila and Nueva Leon, the only Mexican official who had promised anything in writing.[20]

While Hunter took Tucson and Pesqueira "took" Reily, Canby was desperately trying to resurrect Union military authority in New Mexico. He wrote letters to Washington warning that "The conquest of [New Mexico] is a great political feature of the rebellion. It will gain the rebels a name and prestige over Europe, and operate against the Union cause . . ."[21] All he received in return was the promise of 5,000 troops and a brigadier's brevet for himself. The promises then filtered down into the bureaucratic machinery of the War Department and were lost for the next few months.[22]

Canby was unaware that the commander of the neighboring Department of Kansas, Gen. David Hunter, had learned of the situation in New Mexico from Governor Gilpin of Colorado, and had authorized Gilpin to raise troops for service in New Mexico. Gilpin and his Lieutenant-Governor, Lewis Weld, did not bother to await authority after Sibley started moving up the Rio Grande, and when Hunter's permission to form a regiment arrived one was already organized. De-

[20]Rippy, *op. cit.*, 298-299.

[21]OR I, IX, 634-635, Feb. 28, 1862.

[22]OR I, IX, 364-365, Feb. 28, 1862; OR I, VIII, 628-629. Canby decided to hold Craig with his brigade, since there he controlled Sibley's communications with Dona Ana and Texas. In any case, his troops were in no condition for active campaigning.

spite shoddy equipment, scarce provisions and restless rebel sympathizers (a few were hanged after attacking some unarmed recruits), the 1st Colorado Volunteers (nine infantry companies and Samuel Cook's F Company, of cavalry) was formed and drilled at Denver during the opening months of 1862. John Slough, a gentleman of "noble appearance, but the men seem to lack confidence in him . . . His aristocratic style savors more of eastern society than of the free-and-easy border, . . ."[23] was appointed Colonel, and Sam Tappan, merchant and old campaigner, Lieutenant Colonel. The presiding elder of the Rocky Mountain district of the Methodist Episcopal Church, Rev. John Chivington, was originally slated for the chaplaincy, but when he demanded a command position he won the Major's shoulder-straps. He turned out to be the best soldier in the regiment.[24]

Having sent companies H and B to garrison Fort Wise on the road to Kansas, Slough was ready to move the rest of his command to New Mexico by the end of February. On March 1st, "after one and one half days' convulsive effort we were on the road . . . South, we could imagine rather than see the promised land where battles were to be fought and glory

[23]Hollister, *op cit.*, 47; *MR* 1st Colo. (Nov., 1862); Whitford, *op. cit.*, 75; J. Downing, "On Gory Field," *Santa Fe New Mexican*, Aug. 6, 1906; Howland, *loc. cit.*, Aug. 7, 8, 1906. A group of recruits on a road to Denver parted ranks to let a stagecoach pass; they observed too late that its sides were bristling with guns, with which bushwhackers inside mowed down the confused ranks.

[24]Whitford, *op. cit.*, 147. In 1864, Chivington assured himself an infamous place in history by commanding the 1st Colorado during the Sand Creek Indian massacre. A military tribunal sentenced him to death in 1865 (*Santa Fe Gazette*, Oct. 7th, 1865).

achieved."[25] The infantry, its haversacks bulging with "wormy hardtack and rotten bacon,"[26] the headquarters, and the wagons followed a worn trail, while Company F hovered on the point and flanks as pickets. On the 4th, a staff officer from Fort Union arrived and asked Slough to hurry, but on the 5th and 6th he kept his column at the leisurely pace of fifteen miles a day. But on the 7th the news was received "that the enemy had met and defeated Col. Canby at Calverda [Val Verde] and were rapidly advancing upon Fort Union." That day the regiment traversed forty-two miles![27]

On March 9th Slough ordered all extra equipment and all but four days' rations left behind under a small guard, and packed his men in wagons for the sake of speed. On the 10th a "bitter cold" wind arose and "increased in fury till it became a hurricane,"[28] but with the loss of some mules and horses the regiment pushed on. On the 11th the weary troops passed through the gates and onto the parade ground of Fort Union "with drums beating and colors flying,"[29] where they were welcomed by Colonel Paul, the garrison, and an exile from Santa Fe, Henry Connolly, United States Governor of New Mexico.[30]

[25]*MR* 1st Colo. (Nov.-Feb., 1862); Hollister, *op. cit.*, 45-48.

[26]Howland, *loc. cit.*, Aug. 8, 1906.

[27]Whitford, *op. cit.*, 76; Hollister, *op. cit.*, 46; MR 1st Colo., Co. C (Mar.-Apr., 1862), Co. G (Mar.-Apr., 1862).

[28]*MR* 1st Colo., Co. C (Mar.-Apr., 1862); Waldrip, *op. cit.*, 253-254; Hollister, *op. cit.*, 49.

[29]Hollister, *op. cit.*, 52; Santee, *op. cit.*, 71.

[30]Santee, *op. cit.*, 71.

Once wagons were dispatched to round up the equipment left on the road from Denver, Slough, over Paul's protests of seniority, assumed command of the post, Paul's New Mexicans and Regulars, Capt. J. F. Ritter's four-gun battery and Capt. Ira Clafflin's four mountain howitzers. Convinced that his 1,342 men were enough to whip Sibley, Slough decided to abandon Union and march on Santa Fe, intending either to join battle with the Texans or combine with Canby's command. He turned a deaf ear when Paul told him of Canby's orders to hold Fort Union at all costs. After trying every means of persuasion at his command, Paul washed his hands of the whole affair by detailing the events since Slough's arrival in a bitter letter to the Departmental Commander. "My object . . . is to throw the responsibility of any disaster which may occur on the right shoulders."[31]

The enemy Slough was so eager to meet had meanwhile been sweeping victoriously up the Rio Grande Valley. At Socorro, a day's march north of Fort Craig, the Sibley brigade met a detachment of New Mexican Volunteers Canby had posted there to impede the Texans' advance, but these surrendered as soon as the Confederates appeared. Once a hos-

---

[31]MR 1st Colo., Co. G (Mar.-Apr., 1862); Waldrip, *op. cit.*, 253-254; Pettis, *op. cit.*, II, 104, 108-9; *OR* I, IX, 654. The detachment sent to collect the abandoned equipment, under Lt. J. C. Anderson, had to destroy most of it when the horses to haul it gave out.

Slough's Colorado commission as Colonel was senior to Paul's recently acquired Federal commission, but Slough's Federal Commission, of dubious legality, was junior. Gilpin had no authority to raise a regiment for Federal service despite Hunter's request, and was removed from office without reimbursement for debts he incurred by raising the 1st Colorado on his own credit.

pital for the Val Verde wounded was established at Socorro, Sibley continued his march toward the well-stocked towns of Albuquerque and Santa Fe. The Confederates discovered that many riverside villages were garrisoned by New Mexicans, but these seemed to vie with each other in trying to be first to surrender—even those who "fought" usually panicked or gave up after receiving one light volley. But all was not well for the hungry Confederates, who had learned that even the Rio Grande Valley was too barren to subsist them for any length of time; every day they seemed to march toward Albuquerque and Santa Fe with a little more determination.[32]

The thing that most surprised the Confederates was not the lack of resistance from the militia, but the cool reception extended to them by presumably secessionist citizens. Even men who had voted for secession in the Mesilla convention turned a common cold shoulder toward them. The basic cause was probably the conduct of the rowdy adventurers in the brigade, many of whom fought only for loot. While none of the Confederates were too scrupulous about confiscating the property of known Union men, many of the more experienced brigands protected by the buff and gray of the Confederate cavalry preferred to plunder first and ask the victim about his politics

---

[32]Pettis, *op. cit.,* II, 108; Twitchell, *OSF,* III, 38-39; Waldrip, *op. cit.,* 251; Whitford, *op. cit.,* 70-71. The hasty surrenders of the New Mexicans surprised Canby least of all. His correspondence indicates that he chose them to garrison the towns along the river for the simple reason that there they could do less harm to the Union Regulars and Colorado Volunteers in Fort Craig. He possibly speculated that since they were such a nuisance to him, they might bother the Confederates a bit too—even having them captured seemed better than keeping them at headquarters! Did he hope that they would join the rebels, and ruin their army?

later. Such activity forced many neutrals or good-weather rebels into the enemy camp, and caused ardent Southerners to wonder. It was only during their later retreat that the Texans discovered how unwise their policy had been.[33]

The advance guard of the brigade reached Albuquerque on March 2d, and discovered that the Assistant Union Quartermaster, Capt. H. E. Enos, had failed to destroy many of his stores before retreating. Sibley soon arrived and, to the consternation of all, ordered the $6,000,000 worth of supplies burned. "Why it should have been done I never knew, nor did anyone else, unless it was because our men were getting drunk on the [captured] whiskey and our commander had never been sober . . ." wrote Private Noel,[34] while Capt. Teel was somewhat kinder to the General: "[He] was not a good administrative officer. He did not husband his resources, and was too prone to let the morrow take care of itself."[35]

At Albuquerque, a Confederate flag "was made of a captured United States Flag, raised upon a United States flag-staff, the salute fired by a captured United States battery, and Dixie played by a captured United States band."[36] Pomp and cere-

---

[33]Tittman, *op. cit.*, 129; Whitford, *op. cit.*, 71-72; Waldrip, *op. cit.*, 252.

[34]Hunt, *op. cit.*, 60; Pettis, *op. cit.*, II, 108; Harris, *op. cit.*, 41; Waldrip, *op. cit.*, 251; Noel, *op. cit.*, 61.

[35]Teel, *op. cit.*, II, 700. Sibley blamed the conflagration on the Federals, but the other witnesses universally agree that it started after Sibley arrived, and some say it was by Sibley's order. See *ORCSA,* 180, for Sibley's statement.

[36]*ORCSA,* 196. Probably this and the other flags used by the Texans were not the familiar red squares bearing blue-starred St. Andrew's Crosses so familiar to movie-goers. That flag was only introduced to the Virginia army in October, 1861, and never did "catch on" in the western armies. Probably this was the "Stars and Bars," three broad bars (red, white, red), horizontal, and a blue canton with thirteen stars.

mony did little to fill the stomachs of hungry Confederates.

While Sibley blundered at Albuquerque Governor Baylor also showed that he was all too human. He issued an order to the captains of the Arizona Volunteers, instructing them to invite "the Apaches or any other tribe" to come in for parleys, and then to kill all the adults and enslave all the children "to defray the expense of killing the Indians."[37] Sibley, a man who did possess the virtue of knowing and understanding the savages, evidently was enraged at Baylor's presumption in using federal troops (the Arizona Volunteers were not militia, having been mustered into Confederate service), over whom the governor had no authority, for duty so distasteful to their legitimate commander. Angry notes, touching no subject but full of vituperation, passed between the two, culminating in one sent by Baylor to Sibley on March 17th which contained the Governor's resignation.[38] Somehow the two shortly reached an understanding, and the affair blew over.

When Sibley's entire brigade reached Albuquerque on the 17th of March, he started laying plans for an advance to Santa Fe. Maj. Pyron and 500 men of the 2d and 5th Texas were ordered to secure the Territorial capital itself, while Col. Scurry's 4th Texas and Maj. Powhatan Jordan's[39] battalion of the 7th were sent to a small town southeast of Santa Fe

---

[37] *OR* I, L, pt. 1, 942.

[38] Letter, Baylor to A. M. Jackson, AAG, ANM, March 17, 1862, Baylor Jacket, National Archives. By sending this letter to Sibley and not to Richmond, Baylor was sure he could not lose his job; he was appointed Governor by Davis, and could be removed only by him. Cf. Appendix III: A.

[39] Jordan commanded Sutton's battalion; Sutton died at Val Verde.

called Galisteo. From this strategically located point they could strike an enemy force marching from Fort Union along the Santa Fe Trail on the southern flank, or they could converge with Pyron on the Trail and advance to Fort Union. Green's regiment remained at Albuquerque to guard the Confederate rear from Canby.[40]

Making no attempt to keep their objective secret, Pyron and Scurry marched in the appointed directions, continuing the senseless rapine and pillage that had marked their earlier progress. Reaching Santa Fe Pyron discovered that Maj. J. L. Donaldson, Union Quartermaster for New Mexico, had razed $250,000 worth of supplies and had followed Gov. Connolly's administration-in-exile to the protective walls of Ft. Union. Pyron filled the governmental vacuum by installing ex-Surveyor General William Pelham as Confederate Governor of the Territory of New Mexico.[41]

For some unaccountable reason, Pyron then followed the example given by Sibley in Albuquerque, and fired abundant stores missed by Donaldson during the evacuation. "In less than five days we were suffering the agonies of starvation from our own acts of vandalism."[42] The destruction only served to increase local hostility, already intense because of a pro-

[40]*ORCSA*, 180.

[41]Twitchell, *OSF*, III, 39-43; *OR* I, IV, 639-640; Watford, "Ambitions," 172; Pettis, *op. cit.*, II, 108; Waldrip, *op. cit.*, 252; *MR* 2d Colo., Co. A (Capt. James Ford's company, Independent Colorado Volunteers, was part of Donaldson's garrison at Santa Fe. It was later mustered into the 2d Colorado Volunteers, along with Dodd's company, which became Company B of the 2d Colorado.)

[42]Noel, *op. cit.*, 62.

clamation issued by Pyron ordering everyone to swear allegiance to the South or have their property confiscated.[43]

The Confederate soldiers, aware that Sibley had been Fort Union's commander for some time and was therefore well acquainted with its strengths and weaknesses, expected to take the post, and for all practical purposes, New Mexico, in a few weeks' time. They and their officers were completely unaware of the new, stronger fortifications Col. Paul had built near the old site during the previous fall.[44] Few if any imagined that they would never see Fort Union, except as prisoners, and that Sibley's brigade would be expelled from the Territory by the end of July. While they gloried in past victories, various elements of chance, internal discord and Union determination were dovetailing to produce catastrophic defeat for the Texans. Supplies were dangerously low. The civilian population was cool and, on occasions, hostile. Sibley's communications with Texas were constantly threatened by Fort Craig's garrison, which was being rebuilt (again) into a fine brigade by Canby. Worst of all, there were appearing in the Confederate army the first signs of collapsing discipline—the rumor had spread, and was generally believed, that Sibley's sickness at Val Verde was part of a deliberate plot to turn the brigade over to the Federals![45]

Pyron, however, had no time to notice the sullen disposition of his men, for he was occupied with reports indicating

---

[43]Waldrip, *op. cit.*, 252.

[44]Whitford, *op. cit.*, 72, 93-94.

[45]*ORCSA*, 180; Waldrip, *op. cit.*, 253; *OR* I, III, 793 (Col. Steele to Gen. S. Cooper, AG, CSA, March 7, 1862.)

that a regiment of Colorado Volunteers had reinforced the garrison at Fort Union. He felt confident of success when he ordered Maj. J. S. S. Shropshire's battalion of the 5th Texas and Capt. John Phillips' company of Arizona Volunteers to start marching eastward toward Union over the ancient dust of the legendary Santa Fe Trail. Unknown to the Confederates Col. Slough had been aware of their presence in Santa Fe for some time, and, having stripped his equipment to essentials and having drilled his men constantly, he ordered them westward along the same road on the 22d of March.[46]

Half-way between the two commands was La Glorieta Pass.

---

[46]*ORCSA*, 180-181; Harris, *op. cit.*, 45; Hollister, *op. cit.*, 54; Howland, *loc. cit.*, Aug. 8, 1906; Santee *op. cit.*, 71, *et al.*

CHAPTER **IV**

COLONEL SLOUGH WINS A BATTLE

OPING TO arrive in Santa Fe at night and surprise the rebels before they could fight, Colonel Slough pushed his men along the dusty trail, past abandoned pueblo cities and a mission or two, hour after exhausting hour. Late on the 24th of March his 1,300 men reached Bernal Springs, where a bivouac was established a day's march from the mountain pass at Glorieta.[1]

Situated on the Pecos River near the southern end of the Sangre de Cristo range, rugged Glorieta was one of the traditional routes of the American Southwest. Apache, Spanish and American frontiersmen followed each other through it, but even they were latecomers, for ages before its dust had been stirred by the pre-Columbian Mexicans. The elevated, corridor-like pass, clothed in a rich growth of beautiful cottonwoods and pine trees, was several miles in length and a quarter mile wide at the center, but it tapered to narrow de-

---

[1]Santee, *op. cit.*, 71; Harris, *op. cit.*, 44; Watford, "Ambitions," 184; *OR* I, IX, 534-535.

files through the hills at each end. The narrower western end of the valley was sometimes called Apache Cañon.[2]

Early on the 25th, Maj. Chivington and a forward guard of 418 men marched toward the pass, and that evening made camp at Kozlowski's Ranch, guarding its eastern entrance. A picket party of twenty men was sent into the cañon itself early on the 26th to check rumors that a party of Texan scouts was somewhere in Glorieta. At dawn the Federals discovered and captured four rebels near Pigeon's Ranch, a stagehouse near the eastern end of Apache Cañon. One of the crest-fallen prisoners, named McIntire, was later recognized as a man who had been an officer on Canby's staff at Fort Craig until the battle of Val Verde![3]

Now that Chivington had definite information that the rebels were near, he broke camp at 8:00 a.m. on March 26th and advanced cautiously into the pass. About 2:00 p.m. his skirmishers struck a heavy thicket, from which were flushed a Confederate detachment of thirty men and two officers. While the Federals rounded up the prisoners and congratulated themselves on their first tactical victory, artillery bombs began bursting among them. Pyron's main force had arrived.[4]

---

[2]Santee, *op. cit.,* 66; Waldrip, *op. cit.,* 255. Apache Cañon and Glorieta Pass are still major transportation routes; it is possible to see the battlefield from the windows of cars on the Santa Fe Railroad, which passes through the cañon.

[3]Santee, *op. cit.,* 71; *OR* I, IX, 677-680; Harris, *op. cit.,* 44; Whitford, *op. cit.,* 82; Hollister, *op. cit.,* 59. The owner of Pigeon's, Alex Valle, was said to dance like a pigeon—hence the name.

[4]Hollister, *op. cit.,* 59-61; Whitford, *op. cit.,* 84-85; *OR* I, IX, 677-680 Martin Kozlowski, owner of Chivington's camp-site, was amazed at the good conduct of the Volunteers; he had been an old United States dragoon himself.

Colonel Slough Wins a Battle

The Confederates, unawares, had blundered into the Federals, but as soon as Pyron grasped the situation he ordered Lt. James Bradford to unlimber two howitzers on the road, and aligned his dragoons near them. The first rounds threw the Colorado Volunteers into confusion, but they realigned like Regulars at the direction of their officers. A preliminary attack by the Union cavalry gave Chivington time to send detachments of infantry into the wooded hills overlooking the flanks of the Confederate position, and when the cavalry was beaten back the Federal infantry poured such a withering fire into the Texans that they were forced to retreat. These tactics were repeated twice more with equal success, until the rebels took a final position across a sheer defile at the western end of Apache Cañon. Again Chivington sent his infantry into the hills, but, as they cut down the Confederates with a withering enfilade fire, the Major sent Company F of the 1st Colorado, a mounted unit, across an unbridged arroyo and against the very muzzles of the enemy's cannon. The Texans limbered their guns and fled, while the victorious Colorado troops rounded up forty or fifty prisoners, forty-three rebel wounded, and left thirty-two enemy dead where they had fallen. In comparison, the Federal loss was only five killed and fourteen wounded. The best characterization of the way the supposedly "green" Colorado Volunteers fought was contained in a description of Major Chivington by the owner of Pigeon's Ranch: "E poot 'iz 'ead down and foight loike a mahd bool."[5]

---

[5]For the tactics, cf, Hollister, *op. cit;* Whitford, *op. cit;* Downing, *loc. cit.,* Aug. 6, 1906; *OR* I, IX. The quotation appears in Whitford, *op. cit.,* 91, and

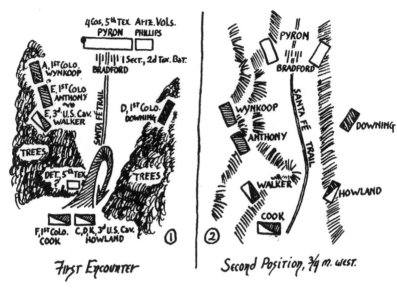

① First Encounter

4 Cos. 5th Tex. Ariz. Vols.
PYRON   PHILLIPS

1 Sect., 2d Tex. Bat.
BRADFORD

A, 1st Colo. WYNKOOP

E, 1st Colo. ANTHONY

E, 3d U.S. Cav. WALKER

D, 1st Colo. DOWNING

SANTA FE TRAIL

TREES

DET. 5th TEX

TREES

F, 1st Colo. COOK   C, D, K, 3d U.S. Cav. HOWLAND

② Second Position, ¾ m. west.

PYRON
BRADFORD
WYNKOOP
ANTHONY
DOWNING
SANTA FE TRAIL
WALKER
HOWLAND
COOK

THE BATTLE OF APACHE CAÑON

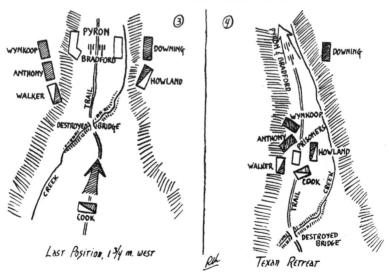

③

WYNKOOP
PYRON
BRADFORD
DOWNING
ANTHONY
HOWLAND
WALKER
TRAIL
DESTROYED BRIDGE
CREEK
COOK

Last Position, 1¾ m. west

④

DOWNING
PYRON & BRADFORD
WYNKOOP
ANTHONY   PRISONERS
WALKER   HOWLAND
COOK
TRAIL   CREEK
DESTROYED BRIDGE

Texan Retreat

Colonel Slough Wins a Battle

Because night was falling Chivington did not pursue the rapidly retreating Confederates, but withdrew to Pigeon's Ranch in order to procure water for his men and horses. During the night two companies arrived at Pigeon's with news that Slough's main column could be expected late on the 27th of March. When that day dawned Chivington sent out burial details to the scene of the battle of Apache Cañon and detachments of foragers to collect the flour and corn abandoned by the rebels in their flight. After breakfasting his men on the Confederate provisions he ordered them back to Kozlowski's Ranch at the eastern end of Glorieta, since the water at Pigeon's had proven insufficient.[6]

Meanwhile, Pyron had gathered together his battered command at Johnson's Ranch, at the western end of Apache Cañon. During the battle he had sent a hurried note to Colonel Scurry at Galisteo, fifteen miles south of Glorieta, and now that the battle was lost he had no choice but to wait reinforcements from the 4th Texas.[7]

Within ten minutes after receiving Pyron's note Scurry had his column formed and marching for Johnson's Ranch. The extreme cold of the night of the 26th-27th March made progress difficult, as cannon and wagons often had to be dragged over the bad mountain trails manually, but disre-

---

is represented as a transcription of Valle's remarks, in his French accent, to a soldier after the fight. Others remembered the sight of Chivington, dressed in full regimentals, cocking and firing two pistols in front of the line, oblivious to danger.

[6]Downing, *loc. cit.,* Aug. 6, 1906; *MR* 1st Colo. (Mar.-Apr., 1862) ; Hollister, *op. cit.,* 67 ; Whitford, *op. cit.,* 96-97.

[7]*ORCSA,* 186.

garding hardship Scurry hurried his men and brought them to Pyron's camp at 3:00 a.m., March 27th. Since Pyron had arranged a temporary truce with Chivington, Scurry allowed his men to rest while he made a thorough examination of the ground. Then, at dawn, he formed his troops to command every approach to Johnson's Ranch, and waited for the Federals to appear. "In this position we remained until the next morning."[8]

While Scurry waited for Chivington to do something, and while Sibley's barber watched the Commanding General stagger around the streets of Santa Fe under the influence of enough whiskey to forget that there was a war going on, Chivington waited for Slough. The Colonel finally arrived with the rest of his brigade at Kozlowski's about 4:00 a.m. on March 28th and, having assumed command, readied his men for battle. Before dawn, he detached seven companies under Chivington and sent them into the mountains to the south, ordering them to march westward and, if possible, fall on the enemy's rear. When this battalion had gone, Slough took his remaining 600-odd men and advanced cautiously into Glorieta Pass.[9]

Scurry had long since become bored waiting for the Federals to attack, and as a result he started moving toward Slough at about the same hour. Unlike Slough's, his 1,100 men were almost all veterans looking forward to another tri-

[8]*ORCSA*, 186-187.

[9]Waldrip, *op. cit.*, 254; Twitchell, *Leading Facts &c.*, II, 384n; *MR* 1st Colo. (Mar.-Apr., 1862); Hollister, *op. cit.*, 68; *ORCSA*, 187.

Colonel Slough Wins a Battle

umph. They advanced carefully until, about 8:30 a.m., they met the first Union skirmishers near Pigeon's Ranch.[10]

The Federals, who had stacked arms at the Ranch and were enjoying a moment of rest, were startled into confused activity when their pickets came running back yelling about massed rebels less than 800 yards away. When Lt. Bradford's two spunky little howitzers started lobbing grape-shot and shell into the Union camp the Federals made a common rush for rifles—the nearest one would do—and, running and tumbling into a slight depression, formed a shaggy battle-line.[11]

Scurry formed a battle line of dismounted dragoons from one wooded wall of the cañon to the other, astride the Santa Fe Trail, and threw his cannon forward in the center. Pyron held the right, Maj. Ragnet the center, and Scurry himself commanded the left. Slough meanwhile put Ritter's and Claflin's eight field-guns across the road in his center, supported by infantry, and ordered other infantry into the woods on either side. He held his cavalry in reserve near the center of the line.

An attempt to outflank the Confederates by sending Lt. Charles Kerber's I Company of the 1st Colorado forward under cover of an irrigation ditch was repulsed with heavy loss by Scurry's wing of the rebel line. Slough did succeed in battering the Confederate artillery into impotence with his

[10]*ORCSA*, 187; Whitford, *op. cit.*, 98-99; Santee, *op. cit.*, 73. In his report Scurry claims he only had 600 men, which, if one fails to count Pyron's 500, is true.

[11]Whitford, *op. cit.*, 102; Harris, *op. cit.*, 47; Hollister, *op. cit.*, 68; Howland, *loc. cit.*, Aug. 8, 1906.

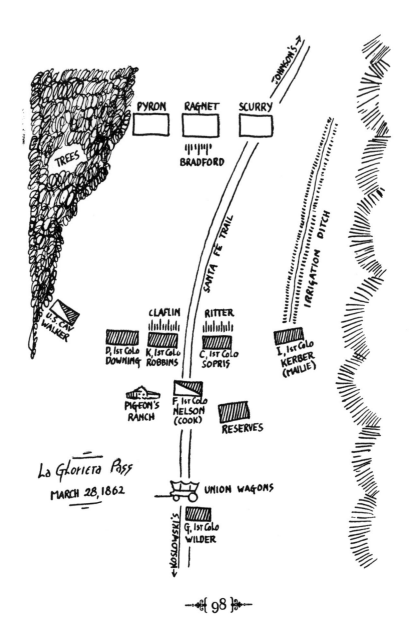

PYRON   RAGNET   SCURRY

JOHNSON'S →

TREES

BRADFORD

SANTA FE TRAIL

IRRIGATION DITCH

U.S. CAV
WALKER

CLAFLIN   RITTER

D, 1st Colo
DOWNING

K, 1st Colo
ROBBINS

C, 1st Colo
SOPRIS

I, 1st Colo
KERBER
(MAILIE)

PIGEON'S
RANCH

F, 1st Colo
NELSON
(COOK)

RESERVES

La Glorieta Pass
MARCH 28, 1862

UNION WAGONS

KOSLOWSKI'S →

G, 1st Colo
WILDER

own heavier guns, but he was unable to shatter the massed Confederate infantry. In fact, Scurry's dragoons pressed forward and obliged the Union artillery and infantry to give ground.

Then Scurry, borrowing some tactics from Chivington, sent flankers into the woods on either side of the Federals. While they harassed the Union cannoneers with musketry the main body of Confederate infantry, "with the brim[s] of their slouched hats falling over their foreheads, and with deafening yells, . . . charged impetuously down the road and its sides towards Ritter's and Claf[f]lin's batteries . . ."[12] The two battle lines struck and intermingled, and ramrods and rocks became weapons of war. Cannoneers rammed in charges with their arms, and amidst the rattle of musketry, the clatter of sabres and the shouts of men, the eight Union guns "played the liveliest Yankee Doodle ever heard—and all the time, thud, thud, thud, the bullets coming down off the mountains on each side into the ground."[13]

Five times the lines swayed back and forth; now the cannon would be dragged back a few yards, now the Confederates would withdraw for a breath. Pyron's horse was blown up under him; Scurry was twiced grazed, but kept to his saddle; Ragnet was killed at the head of his battalion; Lt. Col. Tappan of the 1st Colorado "sat on his horse . . . leisurely loading and firing his pistols as if rabbit hunting."[14]

---

[12]Whitford, *op. cit.*, 111.

[13]Hollister, *op. cit.*, 71.

[14]*Ibid.*, 70.

FORWARD!

Colonel Slough Wins a Battle

In the confusion, Slough's battery supports came to the front and delivered six quick, withering volleys into the Confederate ranks. Then, charging with the bayonet, they forced the Texans westward along the road for some distance, before returning themselves to the Union front. But the enfilade fire from Texas sharpshooters in the surrounding hills nullified the temporary advantage gained by Slough, and, as dusk approached, he fell back with his command and wagons to Kozlowski's Ranch. Scurry regained the ground lost in the last countercharge, and prepared to bivouac at Pigeon's Ranch.[15]

Slough's men were bitter about the defeat, and some officers feared mutiny. Then a carriage bearing a blindfolded man in the full regimentals of a Confederate major swung into camp, and the Federals temporarily forgot their dissatisfaction as they crowded about the ambulance and the major's escort of Union cavalrymen. The rebel—Major A. M. Jackson, Sibley's Assistant Adjutant-General—was led to Slough, held a short conference with him, arranged a truce, and left

---

[15]One interested in the tactical details of Glorieta might check these sources: Hollister, *op. cit.;* Whitford, *op. cit.; ORCSA; OR* I, IX; Downing & Howland, *loc. cit.,* Aug. 6-8, 1906; Santee, *op. cit.;* Harris, *op. cit.; MR* 1st Colo. (Mar.-Apr., 1862); Brannon, Grace, "Battle of Glorieta," Musuem of New Mexico Library Vertical File, Santa Fe, 1935; Stuart, W. S., "The Battle of Glorieta," Museum of New Mexico Library Vertical File, Santa Fe, undated (1933?); Seay, R. T., "Incidents of Glorieta Battle ..." *Santa Fe New Mexican,* Aug. 13, 1906; Paul I. Wellman, *Glory, God and Gold,* Mainstream of America Series, ed. Lewis Gannett (Garden City, N. Y.. 1954) (a decent, available popularization). The maps of Apache Cañon and Glorieta Pass presented in these pages will give the reader an idea of the tactics employed. Glorieta probably has the distinction of being the most out-of-the-way battle of the American Civil War. Skirmishes were fought further west, but 2,000 men, as engaged here, rate it as a small "battle."

the Union camp as quickly as he had come. When the reason for Jackson's mission became generally known, the Union soldiers' curiosity turned to joy. Without realizing it, Slough's brigade had won the Battle of Glorieta Pass!

While Scurry and Slough had been fighting at Pigeon's, a disaster had befallen the Confederates. Chivington's seven Union companies, detached from the brigade early in the morning by Slough, had swung around the entire Confederate command and, under the guidance of Lt. Col. Manuel Chavis of the 1st New Mexico Volunteers, had reached an eminence overlooking Johnson's Ranch about 1:30 p.m. When Chavis looked into the cañon below, he remarked unbelievingly to Chivington, "You are right on top of them."[16] Below, guarded only by a small detachment of Confederates, was Scurry's entire wagon train—mules, horses, ammunition, provisions, sick and wounded, and the hospital stores. Fearing to trust his luck too far, Chivington ordered his men to stay concealed while he, Chavis and Capt. W. H. Lewis of the Regulars examined every foot of the terrain in the valley. Over an hour passed before the order was given: "In single file, double quick, charge!"[17]

It was one of the weirdest charges in history. The Federals first let themselves over the edge of the precipice and down

---

[16]Whitford, *op. cit.*, 116.

[17]*Ibid.*, 117. Lewis was somewhat impatient to get the fight started, and kept trying to hurry Chivington, but the peculiar terrain obliged the Major to know where he was going, and he had to know how many rebels were in the camp. Also, he gave his men an hour's rest by taking his time; they had been marching since dawn.

Rev. John M. Chivington COLONEL, U.S.V.

the sheer walls of a cliff on long ropes and straps, and when they neared the bottom they let go and fell, slid, crawled or tumbled down a boulder-covered gravel drift to the floor of the valley. On the way down they were bothered but not hurt by a badly-served six-pounder which the Confederate guard hastily brought into action.

Forming ranks, the Nationals charged the wagon park, spiked the little rebel gun, and chased the panicky teamsters and guards down the road toward Pigeon's Ranch. Then Scurry's seventy-three wagons, containing everything from grape shot to officers' drawers, were overturned and fired. About 500 to 600 horses and mules corraled nearby were bayoneted, five Union prisoners were freed, and seventeen rebels, including two officers, were rounded up. The only casualties were the Rev. L. H. Jones, a chaplain with the 4th Texas, who was wounded when he ran into someone's line of fire waving a white flag, and a Union private who happened to be too near an ammunition wagon when it exploded.

During the raid a lone rebel courier galloped into the clearing, reined up, took a look, turned his horse and disappeared unmolested in the direction of Pigeon's Ranch. It was probably he who told Scurry of the disaster at Johnson's Ranch.

About nightfall Chivington started his men back toward Kozlowski's. One Father Ortiz, a Catholic missionary, directed them in the darkness and helped them reach their destination by 10:00 p.m. When the exhausted troops fell asleep that evening they had reason to be proud of their tactical *coup,* for it was the military turning point in the campaign for New Mex-

Colonel Slough Wins a Battle

ico. Scurry's request for a truce was a direct result of the catastrophe, for he found that he was unable to control his soldiers when the rumor somehow started that the garrison from Fort Craig, under Colonel Canby, had bypassed Green at Albuquerque and had fallen on the Confederate rear at Johnson's. Even the truth, when it shortly became known, was horrible enough! The 4th Texas and Pyron's battalion were without any supplies whatsoever. As one Confederate private wrote, Glorieta was "where Sibley's Brigade met its Waterloo."[18] Few of the Texans realized that the worst was yet to come.

After remaining at Pigeon's two days, without blankets, tents, food, artillery ammunition, or hospital stores, and with only ten cartridges per man, the demoralized Confederates left their thirty-six dead unburied and their sixty wounded where they had fallen and streamed back, utterly without order, to Santa Fe. Some few Samaritans remained behind to care for the casualties, and luckily found some sacks of flour and baled buffalo meat left in the area by the Indians. "I found a hen beginning to set on 13 eggs. The hen made soup and those eggs fed those poor fellows nearly a week. . ."[19]

Slough did not pursue the Confederates immediately, since his men were just as exhausted as the enemy. When, shortly, the 1st Colorado was ready to march on Santa Fe, a courier

[18]Hollister, *op. cit.*, 71, 72; Whitford, *op. cit.*, 115-122; Downing, *loc. cit.*, Aug. 6, 1906; *OR* I, IX, 538; *ORCSA*, 189; Waldrip, *op. cit.*, 256; Harris, *op. cit.*, 47-50; *MR* 1st Colo. (Mar.-Apr. '62); Anderson, *op. cit.*, II, 699; Noel, *op. cit.*, 60 (quotation).

[19]*OR* I, IX, 533; Pettis, *op. cit.*, II, 109; Miller, *op. cit.*, I, 360; Whitford, *op. cit.*, 126; Wright, Letter; Brannon, "Battle of Glorieta," p. 12.

arrived from Canby ordering Slough to return to Fort Union, where he should have been all along. Obeying orders, Slough reached Union on April 2d—and then, on the 5th, another letter came instructing the regiment to march southward to join the garrison from Craig, which was finally moving north. Sibley was in the middle.[20]

Stranded a thousand miles from its San Antonio base, with one enemy coming from Fort Craig, another from Fort Union, and the ever dangerous Apache and Navajo hovering about its flanks, the Sibley brigade was indeed in a precarious position. Ever since the publication of Baylor's "extermination order" the Indians' animosity to the Confederates had grown, but, luckily, they still refrained from starting a general war against the gray-uniformed "longknives" because of the peace signs Sibley had left along his route since leaving San Antonio. However, the sachems could not restrain every young buck who wanted a Confederate scalp for his very own, and "incidents" were reported with increasing frequency.[21]

After raiding the local merchants of Santa Fe for clothing and provisions, the Confederates abandoned the town on the 5th-6th of April and moved down the Rio Grande, foraging upon the poverty-stricken inhabitants as they went. Sibley abandoned his sick and wounded in the Territorial capital, but provided the citizens with $1,000 in Confederate money to pay for their care.[22]

---

[20]Santee, *op. cit.*, 74; Hollister, *op. cit.*, 73-74, 78.

[21]Noel, *op. cit.*, 59-60.

[22]Seay, *loc. cit.*, Aug. 13, 1906; Whitford, *op. cit.*, 128; Howland, *loc. cit.*, Aug. 8, 1906; *ORCSA*, 183. About all the hungry Confederates were able to

Colonel Slough Wins a Battle

The chief reason Sibley abandoned Santa Fe so quickly was news that Canby was threatening Green's regiment at Albuquerque. On the 1st of April Canby had left Fort Craig with the garrison, and on the 8th he appeared outside Green's hastily-built fortifications ready to besiege the town. On the 8th and 9th he made sorties against the Confederate works and bombarded the houses they enclosed, and then, before Sibley could arrive with reinforcements for Green, the Union brigade evacuated its trenches and melted into the hills as swiftly and as silently as it had arrived. Proceeding via Carnuel Cañon and the village of San Antonio, where Paul's Regulars and New Mexicans from Fort Union joined him, Canby marched to Tijeras where, on the 12th and 13th of April, the 1st Colorado arrived. Since leaving Fort Union this regiment had made a detour to Glorieta, to insure that no rebels were still lurking in the area. There Company F was detached and sent to Santa Fe, to reclaim the capital and re-establish Federal authority there. In Santa Fe the Union soldiers discovered, but did not molest, about 250 rebel sick, wounded, and stragglers, as well as a (lamentably) half-empty case of champagne bottles in Sibley's headquarters.[23]

"liberate" from the bare shelves of Santa Fe's general stores was a collection of artistically executed Indian blankets. Since rebel soldiers often wore blankets like ponchos, it can be imagined that, for the next couple of weeks, the Sibley brigade was the most gayly-uniformed army of the war.

[23]*ORCSA*, 181; Watford, "Ambitions," 185; *Conduct of the War*, III, 368; Pettis, *op. cit.*, II, 110; Whitford, *op. cit.*, 128-129; *MR* 1st Colo., Co. G. (Mar.-Apr., 1862); Howland, *loc cit.*, Aug. 8, 1906; Hollister, *op. cit.*, 82-88; Twitchell, *Leading Facts &c.*, II, 384. Canby did not disturb the rebel hospital in Santa Fe for two weeks, when some officers from it came asking for food. He sent food and attendants then, in return for the surrender of the inmates.

Before arriving at Canby's camp Col. Slough, who had submitted a resignation because of Canby's refusal to let him follow the Texans after Glorieta, turned the 1st Colorado over to Lt. Col. Tappan. However, the officers of the regiment petitioned to have Maj. Chivington appointed commander, and Canby breveted the minister Colonel of Volunteers on April 14th.[24]

Sibley's command, lacking provisions in a land where, by then, the wary civilians had hidden everything of value, lacking money (except for scant amounts of Confederate paper nobody would accept), and too weak to advance against the combined garrisons of Forts Union and Craig, had but one course to follow: retreat. "Accordingly, [Sibley] determined upon retreating from the territory if Canby would allow him to do so."[25] With the sour-grapes attitude that the stores at Fort Union were "scant . . . at the best,"[26] he ordered the brigade to strip to essentials in order to expedite the withdrawal. Eight of Teel's brass howitzers, which were without ammunition anyway, were dismounted and buried in the slime of the Rio Grande's bed, while their carriages were retained for transportation. This left the brigade only two sections of

---

[24]Hollister, *op. cit.,* 74, 86; Santee, *op. cit.,* 75; Resignation, Mar. 31, 1862, Slough Jacket, National Archives; Petition, undated, Chivington Jacket, National Archives. By resigning, Slough turned down a brigadier's commission offered by Lincoln for the Glorieta victory; had he accepted, he would have outranked Canby.

[25]Pettis, *op. cit.,* II, 110.

[26]*ORCSA*, 181-182.

their own artillery and the heavier pieces they had captured from McRae at Val Verde.[27]

On the 12th of April Sibley crossed Scurry's 4th Texas and Pyron's and Jordan's battalions to the west bank of the river. The artillery soon followed, but Green's regiment was unable to find the ford assigned to it and on the 13th was obliged to march down the eastern bank of the river. On the 14th it reached Governor Connolly's ranch at Los Lunas, about twenty miles below Albuquerque and a mile from the sleepy little adobe village of Peralta. There it prepared to bivouac, unaware that the Union army was only a few short miles away.[28]

About midnight, April 14th-15th, Canby's combined brigade made camp a mile from Connolly's Ranch. As soon as the Federals were settled they captured the rebel pickets "as usual" and learned of the enemy's strength and disposition through spies sent across the lines. Intelligence indicated that the rebels thought Canby's forces were somewhere around Galisteo, and that the Texan officers had left the men to fend for themselves while they went into Peralta to attend a fandango.[29]

Chivington suggested that the Federals might overwhelm Green in a night attack before a defense could be prepared,

---

[27]Whitford, *op. cit.,* 130; Harris, *op. cit.,* 52. Three decades later Teel supervised the recovery of four of these abandoned cannon, which were on display at Albuquerque until contributed as scrap in World War II. Since they were not used, Albuquerque is presently trying to recover them.

Whitford is in error when he states Sibley had six guns belonging to McRae; he had only four.

[28]*ORCSA,* 182; Whitford, *op. cit.,* 130.

[29]Hollister, *op. cit.,* 89-91.

but Canby vetoed the proposal "saying that he had not the commissary to take care of them if we took them prisoners, and I think now he was right."[30]

Any chance for a surprise attack was destroyed when dawn on April 15th was greeted by a "thrilling reveille" from Canby's musicians, which was acknowledged by Sibley's band in a stirring rendition of "Dixie." Then, as the opposing forces deployed for battle, a straggling train of seven Confederate wagons and one howitzer appeared galloping pell-mell toward the Confederate camp down the road from Albuquerque. Companies H and F of the 1st Colorado dashed forward to capture the wagons, which, when they saw that they would be intercepted, drew into a tight circle, parked, and spawned riflemen onto the ground. But even the howitzer was unable to stop the charging Federals, and within moments the Texans hoisted dirty handkerchiefs on their ramrods and surrendered. When two companies of Regulars came up to help Chivington's men, the wagons were driven into the Union lines and the prisoners dragged their cannon to Clafflin's battery, where Federal artillerists took over and put it to use.[31]

---

[30]*Ibid.,* 91; Downing, *loc. cit.,* Aug. 7, 1906. Downing, the most ardent anti-rebel captain of the 1st Colorado, had suggested the plan to Chivington. His admission that Canby's argument was valid is worth extra consideration in the light of the abuse later heaped on Canby for refusing to destroy the Texans completely.

[31]Hollister, *op. cit.,* 92-93; Whitford, *op. cit.,* 131; *MR,* 1st Colo., Co. H (Mar.-Apr., 1862). The Texans lost: six killed, three wounded, twenty prisoners, seven wagons, one howitzer, fifteen or twenty horses and seventy mules.

Colonel Slough Wins a Battle

Green's regiment fell back to the adobe walls of Peralta while Canby's men occupied Connolly's Ranch. Sibley tried to cross the rest of his brigade from the west bank to reinforce Green, but Scurry's regiment, realizing the desperate situation of the army, mutinied and refused to cross. Sibley himself, with a few troops, forded the river, but when he was notified that he was cut off from Green by Union cavalry he returned to the west bank, leaving Green to fight his own battle.[32]

There was lively action in the afternoon when Graydon's New Mexico cavalry pierced Green's front and rode up and down the street of Peralta firing revolvers at anything gray, but the Texans rallied, expelled the New Mexicans, and retaliated with a heavy artillery barrage directed at Canby's infantry. The Federals pulled back to the cover of a growth of trees and for the rest of the battle, while the Union cavalry galloped somewhat aimlessly "here, there and everywhere," the Union infantry rested in the shade, bothered only now and then by a well-aimed (or wild) rebel shell.[33]

Late in the afternoon Col. Paul advanced one battalion to test the strength of the Confederate line, but when Canby failed to authorize any reinforcements it fell back into its original position.[34]

Some of Canby's soldiers were none too happy with the result of the so-called Battle of Peralta:

---

[32]*MR*, 1st Colo. (Mar.-Apr., 1862) ; Whitford, *op. cit.,* 131; Hollister, *op. cit.,* 98; *ORCSA,* 182; *Santa Fe Gazette,* April 26, 1862.

[33]Hollister, *op. cit.,* 93-94; Whitford, *op. cit.,* 133. Chivington was just missed by a shell that bounded by him inches from his head.

[34]Hollister, *op. cit.,* 94.

"FIRE AT WILL"

Colonel Slough Wins a Battle

> [Peralta] was the most harmless battle on record, putting one in mind of two gamblers colleagued to *do* a greeny, betting and bluffing together with perfect recklessness to bait him, but suddenly finding their judgment when he put his foot into it . . .[35]

Ugly rumors spread that Canby's relations with Sibley, his brother-in-law, were too close to be "proper" under the circumstances of war; the men were disappointed at Canby's tactics and castigated him unmercifully that night. Why had he not surprised the Texans with a pre-dawn attack? Why had he not overpowered them with concentrated assaults of massed battalions during the day?[36] But as time wore on a few soldiers and most officers, realizing that ". . . it was better to drive [the Confederates] . . . to Texas, . . . then [than] to take them prisoners and divide the half rations we were getting,"[37] resigned themselves to the fact that Canby's tactics, however unromantic, were winning the New Mexican campaign, and opposition to the commander declined.[38]

The condition of Sibley's brigade was almost as bad as if it had been whipped. Scurry's regiment was ready to desert to a man, and the whole army was disaffected. Late on the 15th, under cover of a sandstorm, Sibley ordered Green's regiment to cross to the west bank of the river. Then, on the 16th, having abandoned his dead, wounded, much ammunition and thirty-six wagons, and having ordered all personal baggage

---

[35]*Ibid.*, 95.

[36]*Ibid.*

[37]Howland, *loc. cit.*, Aug. 8, 1906.

[38]Anderson, *op. cit.*, II, 699; Downing, *loc. cit.*, Aug. 7, 1906.

thrown out of the remaining wagons, Sibley started his regiments marching southward once again.[39]

Canby occupied Peralta and, to insure that only the best troops would participate in the closing phases of the campaign, ordered his New Mexican Volunteers to garrison Santa Fe, Albuquerque, and the lesser towns of the upper Rio Grande valley. Then, with his Regulars and Colorado Volunteers, he started marching southward along the east bank of the river. On the 17th his column caught up with the Confederates, who were "skedaddling [like] a crowd of urchins who had been caught in a melon patch."[40] "We could see the Texans all day on the other side [of the Rio Grande], three or four miles distant and a little ahead."[41]

Both commands stopped at nightfall and made camp within sight of each other, but while Canby's men slept Sibley's had no rest. In a council of war Colonels Green and Scurry persuaded Sibley that the only hope of salvation lay in flight: the Confederate army should disband and return to Dona Ana in detail. Acting on this suggestion Sibley fired the sixty-two wagons he had left, destroyed a couple of his useless cannon, issued seven days' rations to his men, and readied them to march before dawn. Before the first shafts of morning light pierced the eastern skies, the Confederate brigade melted and

[39]Hollister, *op. cit.*, 96-98; Whitford, *op. cit.*, 132-133; Howland; *loc. cit.*, Aug. 8, 1906; *MR*, 7th Texas, Co. I (Dec. 31, 1862).

[40]*MR* 2d N.M., Cos. A & B (Mar.-Apr., 1862); Hollister, *op. cit.*, 97; Noel, *op. cit.*, 63.

[41]Hollister, *op. cit.*, 98-99.

flowed in diverging rivulets into the hills and deserts to the south.[42]

Though the rebel camp-fires burned brightly well into the new day, the unearthly quiet and stillness across the river indicated to Canby's pickets that something was wrong. Scouts crossed the river and soon returned with the news that the only Confederates left in the abandoned bivouac were sick, wounded or dead. Canby waited long enough to send men and his wife to nurse the helpless Texans, and then started probing after the disintegrating Texas brigade.[43]

It was again obvious to all that he had no intention of destroying the enemy, so some of the vilifiers who had been so active after Peralta resumed their attacks:

> As Sibley waved his farewell from the opposite bank he seemed to say, "Thank you, gentlemen, for your hostile intentions. Doubtless they are sincere, but Canby and I understand each other." These insinuations may do injustice to Canby, but they embody the ideas of the men . . . Vox Populi Vox Dei.[44]

But Canby realized that he was faced with a dilemma. Either he could expel a Confederate army which was still relatively intact while preserving his own army to meet another

---

[42]*MR* 7th Texas, Co. I (Dec. 31, 1862); *ORCSA*, 182-183; Noel, *op. cit.*, 63.

[43]Pettis, *op. cit.*, II, 110; Waldrip, *op. cit.*, 257; *Conduct of the War*, III, 368; Hollister, *op. cit.*, 100. Of Mrs. Canby, Sibley's sister—a Louisiana belle—one Texan wrote: "Mrs. Camby [*sic*] captured more hearts of Confederate soldier[s] than the old general [Canby] ever Captured Confederate bodies."

[44]Hollister, *op. cit.*, 100 (quotation); Pettis, *op. cit.*, II, 110.

invasion, or he could annihilate the Sibley brigade—and weaken his own immeasurably—in a lengthy desert campaign. His objective was to secure New Mexico from any enemy force, not to destroy one.

David Hunter
MAJ-GEN, U.S.A.

John H. Carleton
COLONEL, U.S.A.

John B. Slough
COLONEL, U.S.A

Union Defenders of the Southwest

CHAPTER V

COLONEL EYRE RAISES A FLAG

We walked and staggered along like the reeling, hungry, thirsty
wretches that we were, with no head, nobody to direct or command,
with the bloodthirsty Dog Canyon Apache Indian[s] following in
our wake and scalping the poor unfortunate boys whose blistered feet
and enfeebled frame made it impossible for them to march further.[1]

N O ONE Confederate described the horrible retreat to
Mesilla. Others remembered hacking their ways
through miles of underbrush with axes and Bowie-
knives, or wrote of the terrible, endless heat that bore down
on them as they crossed waterless wasteland. For two hundred
miles the men—here a squad, there a company, somewhere
else a battalion—walked and staggered along, dropping
muskets, cartridge boxes, blankets and treasured keepsakes
all along their paths. Most headed for Texas, but some struck
westward toward Arizona, some for California. Some were
never seen again.[2]

---

[1]Noel, *op. cit.*, 63-64. Noel suggests that Col. Kit Carson had tried to stir
up the Indians against the Confederates.

[2]Howland, *loc. cit.*, Aug. 8, 1906; Pettis, *op. cit.*, II, 111; ORSCA, 183.
Sibley buried a couple more cannon in the wilderness.

The Confederate Invasion of New Mexico and Arizona

After seven days' rations had lasted ten days, the brigade came out of the wilderness and struck the Rio Grande near Fort Thorn, where supplies had been stored in anticipation of its arrival. "The only thing I ever regretted was that the drunken individual who was the cause of all our misfortune was also kept from starving. . . ."[3]

By the 4th of May the brigade had crossed to the east bank of the Rio Grande and was quartered in villages and houses extending from Dona Ana to Fort Bliss, trying to collect the provisions necessary for a further retreat into central Texas.[4]

Meanwhile on April 20th, Canby crossed the river at Lemitar and followed Sibley's trail of harness, rifles, iron ovens, mule carcasses, ambulances, cigars and putrifying corpses. He sent Graydon's cavalry ahead to harass the Confederates, but the New Mexicans only succeeded in rounding up a handfull of stragglers who were only too glad to surrender. At Socorro Canby's main command found seventy-five Texas "convalescents," most of whom were simply allergic to Confederate uniforms.[5]

"We arrived at Gregg [Ft. Craig] the 22d Apl. & went into camp on half rations."[6] By the 24th Canby had fairly well given up pursuit, and his veterans settled down to garrison life, spending their leisure reading a "bushel or two of books" abandoned by the rebels during their retreat.[7]

[3]*ORCSA*, 183; Noel, *op. cit.*, 63.
[4]*ORCSA*, 183.
[5]Pettis, *op. cit.*, II, 111, 106n; Hollister, *op. cit.*, 103-104.
[6]*MR*, 1st Colo., Co. F (Mar.-Apr., 1862).
[7]Hollister, *op. cit.*, 118.

Colonel Eyre Raises a Flag

A few skirmishes with Navajo and Apache bands and parties of bushwhacking whites, and a near-miss with a squad of roaming Texans on May 21st, occupied detachments from Craig through June. By July, when the 1st Colorado departed for Denver, the campaign was over.[8]

Though the immediate threat offered by Canby was therefore removed by late April, the Texans were still faced with problems. Strung out from Dona Ana to El Paso trying to gather food, forage, military stores and clothing from the none-too-cooperative citizens of the Rio Grande Valley, the 2,000-odd underfed, demoralized survivors of Sibley's 3,700 man brigade were indeed in pitiable condition. During May morale was somewhat lifted by the arrival of two skeleton regiments of volunteers from Texas and intelligence that Judge David S. Terry of California was raising 1,500 troops for Confederate service, but when it soon became evident that the latter would never materialize and the former were too weak to justify reopening the campaign against Canby, Sibley realized that, in spite of recent orders from Richmond, Arizona could not be held.[9]

---

[8]*Ibid.*, 123, 126; *MR*, 1st Colo., Cos. C & E (Jul.-Aug., 1862), Co. G (May-June, 1862). During this period of Indian strife the Comanche nation also acted up, and a few of its bucks went hunting *coup*, but a show of force pacified them without much trouble.

In July, when he detached the 1st Colorado, Canby also sent all his New Mexicans (the Craig garrison) to posts farther north.

[9]Pettis, *op. cit.*, II, 111; *MR* 7th Texas Co. I (Dec. 31, 1862); Watford, *CHSQ*, 138-139; Waldrip, *op. cit.*, 262; Davis to Sibley, June 7, 1862 (Rowland, *op. cit.*, V, 271); *OR* I, IX, 717-718; R. E. Lee to P. O. Hebert, May 31, 1862 (*OR* I, IX, 716). Some say Sibley had only 1,500 men left.

The Confederate Invasion of New Mexico and Arizona

Had Sibley known that the Union government had finally thrown all its weight behind Canby, he might have abandoned New Mexico immediately. In May, 1862, the Union Department of War resurrected Canby's request for 5,000 reinforcements and authorized Gen. Hunter to begin mustering a division for New Mexico at Fort Riley, Kansas. Somewhat earlier, in Denver, the ever-generous people of Colorado had initiated enlistment for Col. Jesse H. Leavenworth's 2d Colorado Volunteer Infantry, similarly destined for New Mexico. And in California, Carleton's brigade was ready to move.[10]

An unprecedented winter rainfall and the lack of both supplies and intelligence about Arizona prevented Carleton from crossing the Colorado River with his entire command immediately after the news arrived regarding the capture of Capt. McCleave, Ami White, and the provisions stored at the Pima Villages. Doubtless he would have been even more apprehensive had he known of the reverses sufferd by Canby at Val Verde and along the upper Rio Grande.[11]

However, inclement weather and inadequate stores did not keep him from probing into Arizona with reconnaissance details. During the first week of April Capt. William P. Calloway and a detachment of 272 men, including McCleave's company, crossed the Colorado with orders to open the road to Tucson. About eighty miles east of Fort Yuma, while the

---

[10]*OR* I, VIII, 628, 631, 653-654; *MR* 2d Colo., (Sept. 23, 1862).

[11]Clendenen, *op. cit.*, 37; *OR* I, L, pt. 1, 917, 931-932, 940, 950-951, 958, 746. Carleton was especially interested in McCleave's fate since the two had been comrades-in-arms and close friends for something over ten years.

Colonel Eyre Raises a Flag

Federals encamped, an element of rebel cavalry surprised and drove in a picket post, and then successfully fled into the desert when their pursuers' horses fagged out. The rest of the march was without incident, and Calloway's battalion bivouaced at the Pima Villages on the 12th of April. The docile Pimas provisioned the Nationals generously from their own meager stores, while in council the assembled caciques informed Calloway that Capt. McCleave had been taken to Mesilla and that a party of Confederate scouts, under Lt. John Swilling, was in the immediate area. Calloway sent Lt. James Barrett and twelve men ahead to find the Texans, and on the 14th of April ordered the rest of his battalion to start for Tucson.[12]

On April 15th Barrett stumbled into Swilling's nine-man troop of cavalry at Picacho Pass, and, in a brisk little skirmish, killed or captured all but one of the rebels. Fearing that Swilling was the advance guard of a stronger force, Calloway withdrew all his men to the Pima Villages and on the 19th began fortifying his camp.[13]

On the same day, the second element of the California brigade, seven companies under Col. West, left Fort Yuma for the Pima Villages, while Carleton remained behind to ready the last and largest part of his command for the desert trek. West reached Calloway's camp on the 29th, where reports reached him that Hunter was still in Tucson. He sent a

---

[12]Sacramento *Union*, May 31, 1862; *OR* I, L, pt. 1, 1002-1003; Wyllys, *op. cit.*, 36.

[13]Sacramento *Union*, May 23, 1862; Hunt, *op. cit.*, 90.

report to Carleton asking him to hurry and emphasizing that if Hunter "played bopeep in the neighborhood a while and flickered around the candle a little longer, he might get his wings singed."[14]

But Hunter was convinced by the results of Picacho Pass that he had no hope of holding Tucson. He evacuated it on May 4th and disappeared into Apache country—from which his command, as an organized military unit, never emerged. The last official document regarding it is a letter from Baylor to General Hebert, dated August 19th, asking if the latter had seen Hunter's Volunteers.[15]

Meanwhile, Carleton had received news of Slough's victory at Glorieta shortly before the end of April, and by May he was impatient to leave Fort Yuma and start active campaigning in Arizona. But he was temporarily restrained by the necessity of checking every detail of his supplies and marching orders, for one mistake could spell disaster in the desert. The brigade had to be split into small detachments, to insure that no more than eighty animals reached a given well during a twenty-four hour period, since the wells could water no more. The 200 wagons were split in four divisions, and these split further into elements. Each wagon carried 3,000 pounds, but by far their most precious cargo were the two water kegs each carried on its sideboards. All the rest of the necessary equip-

---

[14]Hunt, *op. cit.,* 90-91, 92; *OR* I, L, pt. 1, 969-970, 1078.

[15]Wyllys, *op. cit.,* 36; Letter, Baylor to Hebert, Aug. 19, 1862, Baylor Jacket, National Archives.

ment, from cartridges to coarse combs, had to be carried by the men, since extra pack-mules would drink too much.[16]

The 1,500 man "Column from California," formed in platoons of twenty or thirty men each, started along the old Butterfield Stage road to Mesilla (via the Pima Villages, Picacho Pass, Tucson, Apache Pass and Dona Ana) in mid-May. A record heat bathed the Arizona desert and, combined with swirling alkali dust, tortured the heavily-laden men and animals as they plodded along. Squads of sweating, swearing cavalry, with their dusty hats pulled low over their eyes and their sabres clanking rhythmically against their saddles, straggled along in ranks as uneven as the land over which their horses trod. Behind them came herds of ever-thinning longhorn beef cattle, hurried along by Mexican *vaqueros* looking for oases of green in the rough cañons and dry basins. On one occasion, a squad of thirsty infantry was willing to drink from a well from which the body of a murdered man had been fished. Some became sick, some died, but the column kept moving.[17]

Carleton reached the Pima Villages on May 24th, and West greeted him with the news that B Company of the 1st California Cavalry had raised the Union flag over Tucson on the 20th. Sending detachments to regarrison Forts Breckenridge and Buchanan, Carleton proceeded with most of his com-

[16]*OR* I, L, pt. 1, 853, 858-859, 1009; Hunt, *op. cit.*, 99, 105.

[17]Downing, *loc. cit.*, Aug. 7, 1906; Clendenen, *op. cit.*, 36-37; *OR* I, L, pt. 2, 136-145; Hunt, *op. cit.*, 104-105.

mand to Tucson, where he established martial law and proclaimed himself Governor of Arizona on June 8th.[18]

Though Tucson was generally docile, about a dozen unreconstructed rebels had to be rounded up and incarcerated. Most of the citizens extended to the Federals the same total indifference with which they had met Hunter's Texans—any rule was preferable to Apache lawlessness.[19]

While provisioning his men for the journey to Mesilla, Carleton sent Expressman John Jones, Sgt. William Wheeling and a Mexican guide named Chavez eastward with orders to establish contact with Canby. Only Jones escaped the Apache's scalping knives, but on June 20th he was captured by some of Col. Steele's Confederate pickets. Though jailed, Jones was able to smuggle word to Canby that Carleton was in Tucson, thus informing Canby not only of the Californians' whereabouts but also of the fact that the Confederates had learned from Jones that they were near.[20]

Jones' intelligence just confirmed a general belief in the rebel army that the South had no hope of holding Arizona. The Indians, especially Navajos, had been becoming increasingly bold; money was non-existent; officers had been resigning *en masse.* Some of the panic had spread to Texas, where

---

[18]Hunt, *op. cit.,* 88, 110; Wyllys, *op. cit.,* 36; Proclamation of Col. J. H. Carleton, June 8, 1862, Carleton Jacket, National Archives. Carleton was obliged to establish "Camp Lowell" outside Tucson for his men, for he found that when they were quartered in town they paid more attention to the local senoritas than they did to their duties.

[19]Wyllys, *op. cit.,* 36-37; Hunt, *op. cit.,* 113.

[20]Clendenen, *op. cit.,* 37; *OR* I, L, pt. 1, 89, 119-120.

Colonel Eyre Raises a Flag

General Hebert had declared martial law on May 30th. Sibley's estimation of the value of New Mexico had been declining ever since he realized he could not hold it, and he had already bowed to the inevitable when Jones' information was relayed to him.[21]

While leaving 400 dragoons under Col. Steele to hold the Mesilla enclave as long as possible, Sibley had evacuated the rest of his brigade by June 17th and had started the weary men toward San Antonio. There was actually very little left for Steele to guard, because, with the mass resignation of civil officials and the habitual postponing of court sessions after April due to the "disturbed" military situation, the Confederate Territorial government for Arizona had long since collapsed.[22]

Four days later, 140 Californians under Col. Edward Eyre left Tucson and started for the Rio Grande. Despite a skirmish with the Apache in which three men were lost and one coyote was shot by a nervous recruit, Eyre reached the gutted ruins of old Fort Thorn on the 4th of July. There, "amid the wildest cheers from the volunteers," the silken folds of Old Glory were unfurled near the bank of the Rio Grande. A few days later Capt. George Howland's company of the 3d United States Cavalry rode up carrying news and greetings from Fort Craig: Canby and Carleton had joined hands.[23]

---

[21]*ORCSA*, 184; Sibley to Gno. Withers, AAG, CSA, June 4, 1862, Sibley Jacket, National Archives; C. Evans, *op. cit.*, XI, 68. Sibley was forced to publish an Indian extermination order as harsh as Baylor's!

[22]Pettis, *op. cit.*, II, 111; *San Antonio Herald*, June 7, 1862; Walker, "Dona Ana," 256.

[23]*OR* I, L, pt. 1, 98, 102, 120-124; Hunt, *op. cit.*, 119.

Col. Steele evacuated Mesilla on the 8th and El Paso on the 12th of July, as soon as news arrived of Fort Thorn's occupation. He somehow managed to salvage $830 in "spoils of war" from Mesilla, but he left behind the dream of a transcontinental Confederacy. Shortly afterwards four companies from Fort Craig proceeded "down to Messiah [Mesilla] . . . We went down there and the enemy was in Texas. They were retreating as fast as possible."[24]

Short of rations, scattered in detachments, lacking mounts and arms, the remnants of Sibley's brigade marched from water-hole to water-hole, desperately trying to find wells which had not been polluted with dead sheep by the Indians. Some men staggered for over two days before finding a clear well; all lost discipline, and the army turned into a mob. No guards were mounted, no rolls called, no formations ordered. Every man thought only of home.[25]

After leaving Fort Davis the Confederates found the Indians more friendly, and it became easier to negotiate for buffalo and antelope meat. Later, wagons of provisions started coming from San Antonio, and then, as the 1,200-1,500 exhausted troops approached the historic town, its whole population came out on the road to offer succor and look for relatives. The organized portions of the brigade reached San Antonio by August 9th, but individual stragglers and bands of

[24]*OR* I, X, 722; Harris, *op. cit.*, 56; Downing, *loc. cit.*, Aug. 7, 1906 (quote).

[25]*San Antonio Herald,* June 21, 1862; Noel, *op. cit.*, 64-65. Though almost everyone threw away their rifles, most retained their iron ramrods to use as spits for cooking biscuits and small animals.

parolees kept drifting in for months afterwards. About half of the command finally reported, while the rest were never seen by their officers again.[26]

As each unit reached San Antonio it was almost immediately furloughed and dismissed for a period sufficient to rest the men and allow them to procure horses. How many of the ragged, lean men knew, as they started on blistered feet toward their homesteads and farms, that their "Sibley Brigade" would never again reunite?[27]

Though Confederate authority along the Rio Grande had evaporated, it was still necessary for the Union army to solidify its jurisdiction. Carleton, who commanded the only force in the area which was still relatively mobile, started the advance guard of his column from Tucson to Mesilla about a week after Eyre raised the flag at Thorn. One hundred and twenty-six men, twenty-two wagons and two howitzers, under Capt. Thomas S. Roberts, proceeded via the Butterfield road deep into Apache country, and on the 15th of July the cannon and infantry reached Apache Pass. There they were ambushed and surrounded by Mimbreno Apache under old Mangas Coloradas and most of the Chiricahua Apache under the Pontiac of the West, Cochise. In this first major battle of the great Apache war that was to decimate the Southwest for a decade, the troops fought desperately for over ten hours, and finally drove off the bewildered savages with their "wagons

[26]Noel, *op. cit.,* 60; Waldrip, *op. cit.,* 260; *San Antonio Herald,* Aug. 9, 1862.

[27]Seay, *loc. cit.,* Aug. 13, 1906; Letter, Pyron to Hebert, July 14, 1862, Pyron Jacket, National Archives.

that shoot." On the 16th Roberts was able to force his way through the pass despite Indian sharpshooters posted in the boulders on every side, and continue toward the Rio Grande.[28]

With his remaining 1,400 men Carleton left Tucson on July 20-23d and marched to Apache Pass where, in order to hold the Apache in check, he ordered a fort (Bowie) to be built. Then continuing the march eastward, he brought the last of his command to Fort Thorn on the 7th of August. Even before all of his men arrived he sent detachments to probe toward El Paso, which surrendered without much display of patriotic indignation when the first Federals arrived. Many stragglers fell into Carleton's hands, as well as twelve abandoned Confederate supply wagons (marked, curiously enough, with the "U. S." of the Old Army). A hastily organized military administration confiscated the property of all known secessionists in the area, including that of Simeon Hart, "a man who did more than anyone else to bring Sibley's force into this country . . ."[29] From El Paso squadrons of cavalry penetrated ever deeper into Texas, captured Fort Quitman without a fight on August 22d, and, a few days later, raised the Stars and Stripes above the walls of Fort Davis. When, in September, Carleton replaced recently-promoted Canby as commander of the Military District of New Mexico, military operations in the Territory had long since concluded.[30]

[28]*OR* I, L, pt. 1, 126-133; Hunt, *op. cit.,* 120.
[29]*OR,* I, IV, 578 (quote); Wyllys, *op. cit.,* 37; *OR* I, L, pt. 1, 772, 94, 110-111, 117; Hunt, *op. cit.,* 127.
[30]*OR* I, L, pt. 1, 102, 44, 116; Extract, Special Orders No. 181, Aug. 5, 1862, Canby Jacket, National Archives.

FLAG, FIRST COLORADO REGIMENT OF VOLUNTEERS

THE END OF BAYLOR'S BATTALION (LETTER)

Colonel Eyre Raises a Flag

But it was still necessary to end civilian unrest. Ever since Governor Connolly had returned to Santa Fe in April, lawlessness had increased as Indians, bandits and "Secesh" citizens tried to fill the power vacuum they supposed had been left by the evacuation of the Confederates. Carleton proved himself a remarkably able military governor, for, before a year had passed, most of the secessionists left in New Mexico were under arrest, towns had been cleared of bandits and companies of loose women, an iron-clad system of passes had been established, an intensive military campaign had pushed the Navajos and Apache back to their citadels in the badlands, and it was possible to travel safely on any of New Mexico's public roads.[31]

District Attorney Joab Houghton proved an able ally to Carleton in his campaign to stamp out the effectiveness of rebel sympathizers. Mass-produced indictments were served against twenty-six prominent citizens by the fall of 1862, accusing them of having "conspired, composed, imagined, and designed to stir up and excite insurrection, rebellion and revolt and to levy war against the government, with Henry H. Sibley and other false traitors."[32] Some of the trials resulting from Houghton's reign of terror dragged on until 1867, though most of the defendants lost their property by confiscation and their popularity by social ostracism long before that date.[33]

---

[31]*Santa Fe Gazette,* April 26, 1862; Clendenen, *op. cit.,* 40-41, *et al.*

[32]Tittman, *op. cit.,* 132.

[33]*Ibid.,* 129-138, for the particulars.

Peculiarly, "Governor" Baylor, who was also indicted by Houghton, received his punishment not from the United States but from the Confederate States government. On the 7th of November, 1862, he received a letter from the Secretary of War informing him that President Davis had just read his order for the extermination and enslavement of the Indians and, being greatly displeased, had ordered Baylor's commission in the army revoked and his appointment as Territorial governor withdrawn. On December 29th Baylor, a private in the Confederate army (in which grade he served in the Galveston campaign of 1863), replied to Davis by way of a letter routed through General John Magruder, in which he explained that the Indians had left him no choice. As if to prove his point, he enclosed in the letter the withered scalp of a Miss Jackson.[34]

Baylor remained a private. With his demotion the sometime Confederate States Territory of Arizona disappeared from the statute books, for a successor was never appointed.

However, the dream to conquer the Southwest did not die as swiftly. A number of proposals to reopen the campaign were made by various persons who used the same arguments first proposed by Sibley and his associates in 1861, and one of these plans, that of Lansford Hastings, received the approval of the Confederate War Department in October, 1863. Other than tentatively appointing a commander (Col. William

---

[34]Harris, *op. cit.,* 58; Wyllys, *op. cit.,* 37; Wellman, *op. cit.,* 317. At the time Baylor received the demotion he was trying to organize a second expedition to New Mexico (Baylor to C. M. Mason, Aug. 25th, 1862, Baylor Jacket, National Archives.)

Steele of the Sibley brigade, who had since become a Brigadier General) for the expedition, the Confederate government
did nothing to carry it out, and by 1864 it was obvious to
Hastings that the emaciated South could support him with
nothing more than words. He turned from his original plan
to various secessionist projects which bore a striking resem-
blance to the Copperhead conspiracy then infesting the Old
Northwest. By 1865, he evidently lost his grip on reality, for
while the granite of the Confederacy's foundations turned to
sand he petitioned Richmond to raise an army to go to South
America and conquer the Empire of Brazil.[35]

The Civil War in the Southwest, devoid of the gigantic
splendor of the struggle in the East, dragged on until 1867,
consisting of a dreary chronicle of marches, Indian fights,
bushwhacking, ambushes, murders, lynchings, desertions and
skirmishes between Union, Confederate, Mexican, Irregular
and "Jayhawker" troops in any possible combination. Even
when the white men made peace the Indians kept fighting,
and men remembered the Sibley brigade and the wreckage it
had left behind until Geronimo surrendered to the United
States army in 1886.[36]

If successful, the conquest of New Mexico might have led
to a Confederacy larger than the Union, a Confederacy able
to marshal two or three more field armies, a Confederacy

---

[35]Wm. Hunsaker, "Lansford W. Hastings' Project for the Invasion and
Conquest of Arizona and New Mexico for the Southern Confederacy," *Arizona Historical Review*, IV (1931-2), 5-12.

[36]D. S. Howell, "Along the Texas Frontier During the Civil War," *West
Texas Historical Association Yearbook*, XIII (1937), 89-95.

with an unblockadable Pacific coast, a Confederacy rich in minerals and able to revivify its sagging economy, a Confederacy recognized as one of the Sisterhood of Nations. Had Sibley won, all this might have come to be. Why did he fail?

The reason was not simply the tactical reverse at Glorieta. Rather, there were a number of major weaknesses in the planning and conduct of the whole campaign which made Glorieta, or some similar engagement, almost inevitable.

Sibley's army was inadequate. His 3,700 men, depleted by sickness, desertion, and the detachment of reconnaissance, foraging and similar parties, were no match for the 12,000-odd troops commanded by Canby, Carleton, Slough, Leavenworth and David Hunter. Not only were statistics against the Confederates, but the fact that they were obliged to wage the whole operation with the same exhausted men while their enemy used fresh reserves in every major engagement tipped the balance in favor of the Nationals.

Secondly, because of the poverty of New Mexico, Sibley could only make his occupation permanent if he was provisioned from Texas or captured abundant stores from the Federals. Canby's and Slough's stiff opposition and Sibley's own wanton carelessness negated the second alternative, while the main Confederate army received nothing from Texas after January, 1862.

The Nationals were as ill-supplied as the Confederates, with one decisive difference. Whereas the same Confederates fought the entire campaign on half rations, each Union detachment was relatively fresh and well provisioned until its first encounter with the enemy. In general, the Union picture was as bleak as the Confederate, while in detail it was much superior.

In the third place, the Texans' poor discipline, stemming partly from their general disinclination to submit to command, partly from Sibley's poor example, and partly from a hatred of New Mexicans that dated to the Compromise of 1850, turned all but the most staunch Arizona secessionists against them. The hostility that greeted them during their retreat stemmed directly from their earlier conduct.

Their distrust of General Sibley was particularly intensive, as shown by the mutiny at Peralta. His intoxication on the days of both Val Verde and Glorieta, and his seeming cowardice during the battles of Val Verde and Peralta, added fuel to the soldiers' antagonism. Where discipline lacks in an army, only personal leadership can afford some measure of efficiency. To a particularly high degree in the psychology of the average Confederate soldier, leadership was almost always equated with the feudal idea of personal courage. By failing to manifest that quality, Sibley was instrumental in defeating his own project.

Finally, while possessing a good, workable strategic plan, Sibley was not tactician enough to carry it out. As did all too many Southern generals he insisted on fighting an 18th century war of position, depleting his command by garrisoning posts along his line of march. Canby, on the other hand, ignored all but the vital positions at Forts Craig and Union, where he concentrated his army for massive blows against the rebels. Yet, realizing his own weakness and supply shortage, Canby was careful never to let his victories be too decisive, since he could not afford to feed a thousand or more prisoners of war. Canby won his strategic objective, the expulsion of the Texans from New Mexico, by pounding away at their ability and will to fight in several inconclusive skirmishes and battles.

Had the Confederates won, later historians might have looked on the campaign in New Mexico as one of the conclusive operations of the Civil War. Without the land, men, agricultural and mineral products, ports and prestige offered by the Southwest, without a rich frontier suitable for later expansion and growth, hemmed in by Mexico, the Union and the sea, the Confederate States of America could carve for itself the position of a secondary American power at best. When its industrial poverty, its decreasing agricultural productivity, its overdependence on cotton and an increasingly uneconomic slave system are taken into account, it appears that the Confederacy had little if any real hope of matching the military might of the colossus of steel and manpower with which it was at war. In the long run this spelled ultimate annihilation for the Southern Republic, because, engaged as it was in a contest allowing no compromise between the antagonistic principles of complete independence or reunification with the North, it could not win without being the North's economic, technological and military equal.

EPILOGUE

(During the retreat of the Texans from Peralta to Dona Ana, Private Ovando Hollister of the 1st Colorado, United States Volunteers, made the following entry, dated April 21st, 1862, in his diary):

Poor Fellows! The climate and Uncle Sam's boys have sadly wasted them. They are now flying through the mountains with a little more than a third of the number with which they first assaulted us at Fort Craig. Many, very many, "softly lie and sweetly sleep low in the ground." Let their faults be buried with them. They are our brothers, erring it may be, still nature will exact a passing tear for the brave deed. And doubt not there are who will both love and honor the memory if we cannot. Any cause that men sustain to death becomes sacred, at least to them. Surely we can afford to pay tribute to the courage and nobleness that prefers death even to *fancied* enthralment.

APPENDICES

Brigade Headquarters

Commanding Officer: Brigadier-General Henry Hopkins Sibley.

Brigade Staff: Major Arthur M. Jackson, Assistant Adjutant-General, Confederate States Army, and Adjutant-Major of Brigade; Major W. L. Robards, aide-de-camp; Captain R. R. Brownrigg; Captain (?) Griffin; Dr. (?) Covey, Brigade Surgeon-General; Lt. Thomas P. Ochiltree, volunteer aide; Joseph E. Dwyer, volunteer aide; Rev. L. H. Joyce, chaplain; Rev. William J. Jones, chaplain.

Second Regiment of Texas Mounted Volunteers, C.S.A.

Commanding Officer: Colonel John Ford.

Staff: Lt. Col. John R. Baylor, Executive Officer; Major Ed. Waller, Major and Adjutant-Major.

(Company)	(Date of Muster)	(Length of Term)	(Commander)
A	May 23, 1861	1 year	Capt. Peter Hardeman
B	May 23, 1861	1 year	Maj. Charles S. Pyron
C	June 25, 1861	1 year	Capt. W. C. Adams
D	May 28, 1861	1 year	Capt. James Walker
E	May 23, 1861	1 year	Capt. D. Le Stafford
F	May 23, 1861	1 year	Capt. Sam. Richardson
H	May 23, 1861	1 year	Capt. N. A. Hammer

(Companies G, I, and K of the 2d Texas were not part of the brigade)

First Regiment of Texas Artillery, C.S.A.

(Company)	(Date of Muster)	(Length of term)	(Commander)
B	May 1, 1861	1 year	Capt. Trevanion T. Teel

The Confederate Invasion of New Mexico and Arizona

Companies of Independent Arizona Volunteers, Attached to the 2d Texas.

Cavalry: Capt. Bethel Coopwood's Company; Capt. G. F. Frazer's Company; Capt. Thomas Helm's Company; Capt. Sherod Hunter's Company; Capt. T. L. Master's Company; Capt. John Phillips' Company.

Infantry: Capt. Jason Davis' Company.

Fourth Regiment of Texas Mounted Volunteers, C.S.A.

Commanding Officer: Colonel James Reily (second in command to Gen. Sibley).

Staff: Lt. Col. William R. Scurry, Executive Officer; Major W. H. Ragnet, Major; Captain (?) Reily, Adjutant-Major; Captain H. E. Loebnits, aide; Captain (?) Nobles, aide; Dr. William Southworth, Regimental Surgeon; Dr. J. W. Mochett, Assistant Surgeon; Dr. (?) Taylor, Assistant Surgeon.

(*Company*)	(*Date of Muster*)	(*Length of Term*)	(*Commander*)
A	Aug. 28, 1861	For the war	Capt. William P. Hardeman
B	Aug. 27, 1861	For the war	Capt. A. J. Scarborough
C	Sept. 11, 1861	For the war	Capt. George J. Hampton
D	Sept. 16, 1861	For the war	Capt. Charles M. Lesueur
E	Sept. 24, 1861	For the war	Capt. Charles Bukholt
F	Sept. 25, 1861	For the war	Capt. Marinus Heuvil
G	Sept. 24, 1861	For the war	Capt. James Crosson
H	Sept. 29, 1861	For the war	Capt. (?) Doherty
I	Sept. 29, 1861	For the war	Capt. (?) Nunn
K	Oct. 4, 1861	For the war	Capt. (?) Ford
Regimental Artillery Section			Lt. John Reily

Fifth Regiment of Texas Mounted Volunteers, C.S.A.

Commanding Officer: Colonel Thomas Green (third in command to Gen. Sibley).

Staff: Lt. Col. Harry McNeill, Executive Officer; Major Samuel Lockridge, Major and Adjutant; Captain Thomas Beck, aide; Lt. Joseph Sayers, aide; Dr. H. Brocht, Regimental Surgeon; Dr. J. M. Broneagh, Assistant Surgeon; Dr. J. H. McPhail, Assistant Surgeon.

(*Company*)	(*Date of Muster*)	(*Length of term*)	(*Commander*)
A	Aug. 29, 1861	For the war	Capt. J. S. S. Shropshire
B	Sept. 2, 1861	For the war	Capt. Willis S. Lang (lancers)
C	Sept. (?) 1861	(?)	Capt. Denman W. Shannon
D	Sept. 3, 1861	For the war	Capt. Daniel H. Ragsdale
E	Sept. 4, 1861	For the war	Capt. H. A. McPhaill

Appendices

Fifth Regiment of Texas Mounted Volunteers, C.S.A. (Continued)

(*Company*)	(*Date of Muster*)	(*Length of Term*)	(*Commander*)
F	Sept. 5, 1861	For the war	Capt. G. W. Campbell
G	Sept. 25, 1861	For the war	Capt. J. B. McGowan (lancers)
H	Oct. 11, 1861	For the war	Capt. Reddin S. Pridgen
I	Oct. 19, 1861	For the war	Capt. Ira G. Killough
K	Oct. 23, 1861	For the war	Capt. Charles L. Jordan
Regimental Artillery Section			(?)

Seventh Regiment of Texas Mounted Volunteers, C.S.A.

Commanding Officer: Colonel William Steele (fourth in command to Gen. Sibley).

Staff: Lt. Col. J. S. Sutton, Executive Officer; Major Arthur P. Bagby, Major; Captain Thomas Howard, Adjutant Major; Captain (?) Ogden, aide; Captain (?) Lee, aide; Dr. George Cupples, Regimental Surgeon; Dr. (?) Greenwood, Assistant Surgeon; Dr. (?) Hunter, Assistant Surgeon.

(*Company*)	(*Date of Muster*)	(*Length of Term*)	(*Commander*)
A	Oct. 4, 1861	For the war	Maj. Powhatan Jordan
B	Oct. 8, 1861	For the war	Capt. Gustav Hoffman
C	Oct. 24, 1861	For the war	Capt. H. M. Burrows
D	Oct. 24, 1861	For the war	Capt. William S. Cleavers
	(Originally an idependent company mustered Sept. 10)		
E	Oct. 23, 1861	For the war	Capt. W. L. Kirksey
	(Originally an independent company; no date for first muster)		
F	Oct. 26, 1861	For the war	Capt. J. F. Wiggins
G	Oct. 26, 1861	For the war	Capt. H. W. Fisher
H	Oct. 28, 1861	For the war	Capt. Isaac Adams (or Adairs?)
I	Nov. 1, 1861	For the war	Capt. James W. Gardner (cashiered) Capt. John W. Taylor
Regimental Artillery Section			Lt. (?) Wood
	(Company K of the 7th Texas was not part of the brigade)		

(These statistics were compiled from the Muster Rolls of the various regiments on file in the Old Army Records Department, National Archives, Washington, D. C.)

The Confederate Invasion of New Mexico and Arizona

II—BATTLE STATISTICS OF THE CAMPAIGN

(The following statistics are presented as a survey of the units involved, numbers, commanders and losses, in the various tactical operations of the New Mexican campaign. The statistics have been compiled from the Muster Rolls of the regiments, official reports published in the *OR* or the *ORCSA*, private letters and other primary sources mentioned in the Bibliography. These statistics, unfortunately, are not complete due to omissions and/or deletions in the available documents.)

(Under "Losses" I have included only those resulting from actual tactical operations. Desertion from both armies was so widespread it is almost hopeless to try and document it.)

The Battle of Fort Fillmore, July 25-27, 1861

Union: Elements, 7th U. S. Cavalry; Elements, 3d U. S. Cavalry; c. 450 men, total, commanded by Maj. Isaac Lynde.

Confed.: 4 cos., 2d Texas Mounted Vols., Lt. Col. John R. Baylor; Battery B, 1st Texas Artillery, Capt. T. T. Teel; 1 co., Arizona Volunteers, Capt. Thomas Helm; 308 men, total, commanded by Lt. Col. Baylor.

Losses: Union, 3 k., 6 w., *ca.* 400 prisoners; Confed.: 0.

Ambush at Picacho (Cook's Cañon), N. M., August (15?), 1861

Union: 4 cos., 7th U. S. Infantry; 1 co., 2d U. S. Artillery; 2 cos., 3d U. S. Cavalry; c. 400 men, total, commanded by Capt. Isaiah N. Moore.

Confed.: Elements, Arizona Volunteers, Capt. Thomas Helm; Elements, Battery B, 1st Texas Artillery, Capt. T. T. Teel; Elements, 2d Texas Mounted Vols., Lt. Col. John Baylor; c. 100 men, total.

Losses: Union, 0; Confed., 0.

Alamosa, N. M., 25-27 September, 1861

Union: (?), total 180.

Confed.: 3 cos., Arizona Vols., 118 men, total, commanded by Capt. Bethel Coopwood.

Losses: Union, 10 killed, ? w.; Confed., 2 k., 8 w.

Indian Expedition, late fall, 1861

Confed.: 1 co., Arizona Vols., c. 50 men, total, commanded by Capt. Thomas Helm.

Indian: Gila River and Chiricahua Apache bands.

Losses: Confed., 50 missing; Indian, (?).

Puero, N. M. December 30, 1861

Union: 1 troop, N.M. cavalry, c. 20 men, commanded by Corp. (?) Avita.

Indian: 1 Navajo war party.

Losses: Union, 1 w.; Indian, 1 k.

Appendices

Skirmish below Fort Craig, New Mexico, February 16, 1862

Union: 1 co., 1st N.M. Vols., Col. C. Carson, c. 60 men.
Confed.: 1 co. (?) Texas cav., c. 50 men.
Losses: 0.

Val Verde, N. M., February 21, 1862

Union: 5 cos., 3d U.S. Cavalry, 2 cos., 2d U.S. Dragoons, Maj. Thomas Duncan; 2 cos., 5th U.S. Infantry, Capt. (?) Wingate; 3 cos., 7th U.S. Infantry, Capt. (?) Plympton; 1 U.S. Provisional Battery, Capt. Alex McRae; 1 U.S. Provisional Artillery Section, Lt. Robert Hall; 1st N.M. Vols., Col. Christopher Carson; 7 cos., 2d N.M. Vols., Col. Miguel Pino; 7 cos., 3d N.M. Vols., 1 co., 4th N.M. Vols., 2 cos., 5th N.M. Vols., Lt. Col. Benjamin Roberts; 1 N.M. Spy (cavalry) Co., Capt. James Graydon; 1 co., Independent Colo. Vols., Capt. William Dodd; About 1000 unorganized N.M. militia; 3810 men, total, commanded by Col. E. R. S. Canby.
Confed.: 4th Texas Mounted Vols., Lt. Col. W. R. Scurry; 5th Texas Mounted Vols., Col. Thomas Green; 5 cos., 2d Texas Mounted Vols., Maj. Charles Pyron; 5 cos., 7th Texas Mounted Vols., Lt. Col. John Sutton; Battery B, 1st Texas Artillery, Capt. T. T. Teel; c. 2600 men, total, commanded by Brig. Gen. H. H. Sibley.
Losses: Union, 68 k., 160 w., 35 m.; Confed., 31 k., 154 w., 1 m.

The Affair at Tucson, Arizona, March (12?) 1862

Union: Element, Co. A, 1st Calif. Cavalry, 9 men, Capt. Wm. McCleave.
Confed.: Element, Arizona Vols., 30 men, Capt. Sherod Hunter.
Losses: Union, 9 prisoners; Confed., 0.

Skirmishes along the Rio Grande, N. M., late Feb., early Mar., 1862

Union: Elements, 1st, 2d, 5th N.M. Vols., ? men.
Confed.: Same as Val Verde, c. 2500 men, total.
Losses: Union, all prisoners or missing; Confed., 0.

Skirmish at Pigeon's Ranch, N. M., March 25, 1862

Union: Troop, Co. F., 1st Colo. Vols., 20 men, Lt. J. Nelson.
Confed.: Squad, Arizona Vols., Lt. McIntire, 4 men.
Losses: Union, 0; Confed., 4 prisoners.

Battle of Apache Cañon, N.M., March 26, 1862

Union: 4 cos., 1st Colo. Vols., Maj. John Chivington; 1 co. plus detachments, 3d U. S. Cavalry, 2 cos., U. S. Cavalry, Capt. Geo. Howland; 418 men, total commanded by Maj. Chivington.
Confed.: 5 cos., 2d Texas Mounted Vols., Maj. Charles Pyron; 4 cos., 5th Texas Mounted Vols., Capt. J. S. S. Shropshire; Section, Battery B, 1st

The Confederate Invasion of New Mexico and Arizona

Battle of Apache Cañon (Continued)

Texas Art., Lt. James Bradford; 1 co., Arizona Vols., Capt. John Phillips; c. 500 men, total, commanded by Maj. Pyron.

Losses: Union, 5 k., 14 w.; Confed., 32 k., 43 w., 71 m.

Battle of Glorieta Pass, N. M., March 28, 1862

Union: 2 cos., 1st U. S. Cavalry, 2 cos., 3d U. S. Cavalry, Elements, 3d U. S. Cavalry, Capt. Geo. Howland; 2 cos., 5th U. S. Infantry, Capt. W. H. Lewis; 3 cos., 1st N. M. Vols., Lt. Col. Gabriel Paul; Regt. Battery, 15th U. S. Infantry, Capt. J. F. Ritter; Regt. Battery, 3d U. S. Cavalry, Capt. Ira Clafflin; 1st Colo. Vols., Col. John Slough; 1 co. Independent Colo. Vols., Capt. James Ford; 1342 men, total, commanded by Col. Slough.

Confed.: 5 cos., 2d Texas Mounted Vols., Maj. Charles Pyron; 4 cos., 5th Texas Mounted Vols., Capt. J. S. S. Shropshire; 4th Texas Mounted Vols., Col. William Scurry; 5 cos., 7th Texas Mounted Vols., Maj. Powhatan Jordan; 1 co., Arizona Vols., Capt. John Phillips; Section, Battery B, 1st Texas Art., Lt. James Bradford; c. 1100 men, commanded by Col. Scurry.

Losses: Union, 31 k, 50-75 w., 30 m.; Confed., 36 k., 60 w., 25 m.

Skirmish 80 miles East of Fort Yuma, Calif. April 2-3, 1862

Union: 2 cos., 1st Calif. Inf., Capt. Nathaniel Pishon; 1 co., 1st Calif. Cav., Capt. William Calloway; Regt. Battery, 1st Calif. Inf., Lt. (?) Phelan; 272 men, total, commanded by Capt. Calloway.

Confed.: Element, Ariz. Vols., c. 15-20 men total, commanded by ?

Losses: o.

Siege of Albuquerque, N. M., April 8-9, 1862

Union: 5 cos., 3d U. S. Cavalry, 2 cos., 2d U. S. Dragoons, Maj. Thomas Duncan; 2 cos., 5th U.S. Infantry, Capt. Wingate; 3 cos., 7th U.S. Infantry, Capt. Plympton; 1 co., 2d U. S. Artillery; 1 N. M. Independent Spy Co., Capt. James Graydon; Elements, N. M. Vol. Inf., Lt. Col. Benjamin Roberts; 1200 men, total, commanded by Col. E. R. S. Canby.

Confed.: 5th Texas Mounted Vols., Col. Thomas Green; 2 sections, Battery B, 1st Texas Art., Capt. T. T. Teal; Elements, Arizona Vols., Capt. Bethel Coopwood; c. 700 men, total, commanded by Col. Green.

Losses: ?

Capitulation of Santa Fe, N. M., April 12, 1862

Union: Co. F., 1st Colo. Vols., c. 95 men commanded by Lt. J. Nelson.

Confed.: Unorganized elements, 2d, 4th, 5th, 7th Texas Mounted Vols., Battery B, 1st Texas Art. and Arizona Vols., c. 250 men, total.

Losses: Union, o; Confed., 250 prisoners.

Appendices

Battle of Peralta, April 15, 1862

Union: 5 cos., 3d U. S. Cavalry; 2 cos., 2d U. S. Dragoons; 2 cos., 5th U. S. Infantry, Capt. (?) Wingate; 3 cos., 7th U. S. Infantry, Capt. (?) Plympton; 1 co., 2d U. S. Artillery, 2 cos., 1st U. S. Cavalry, 2 cos., 3d U. S. Cavalry, Elements, 3d U. S. Cavalry, Capt. G. Howland; 2 cos., 5th U. S. Infantry, Capt. W. H. Lewis; 3 cos., 1st N. M. Vols., Col. C. Carson; Battery, 3d U. S. Cavalry, Capt. Ira Clafflin (Col. Gabriel Paul); 1 N. M. Independent Spy Co., Capt. James Graydon; Elements, N. M. Vols., Lt. Benjamin Roberts; 1st Colo. Vols., Col. John Chivington; c. 2600 men, commanded by Col. E. R. S. Canby.

Confed.: 5th Texas Mounted Vols., Col. Thomas Green; Elements, 2d and 7th Texas Mounted Vols.; Battery B, 1st Texas Art., c. 800 men, commanded by Col. Green.

Losses: ?

Battle of Picacho Pass, Arizona, April 15, 1862

Union: Element, 12 men, Co. A., 1st Calif. Cavalry, Lt. James Barnett.
Confed.: Element, 9 men, Arizona Vols., Lt. Jack Swilling.
Losses: Union, 4 k. and/or w.; Confed., 8 k., w., and/or captured.

Skirmish at Socorro, N. M., April 20, 1862

Union: Element, N. M. Spy Co., Capt. James Graydon, 2 men.
Confed.: Unorganized Element, Texas Mounted Vols., 7 men.
Losses: Union, 0; Confed., 7 prisoners.

Capitulation of Socorro, N. M., April 21, 1862

Union: Same as Peralta, c. 2600 men.
Confed.: Unorganized elements, Texas Mounted Vols., 75 men.
Losses: Union, 0; Confed., 75 prisoners.

Indian Conflict in Arizona, between 4 May-29 August, 1862

Confed.: 1 co., Arizona Vols., c. 90 men, Capt. Sherod Hunter.
Indian: Mimbreno Apache, Mangas Coloradas; Chiricahua Apache, Cochise; Gila River Apache, (?) Total ?
Losses: Confed., c. 90 missing; Indian, ?

Piriji, N. M., May 21, 1862

Union: 5 cos., 1st Colo. Vols., c. 300 men under Capt. William Wilder
Confed.: ?
Losses: 0.

Indian Conflict in New Mexico, May, 1862

Union: Elements, Co. F, 1st Colo. Vols., c. 50 men under Lt. J. Nelson.
Indians: Navajo war parties, Comanche war parties.
Losses: Union, at least 1 k., 1 m.; Navajo, ? Comanche, 0.

The Confederate Invasion of New Mexico and Arizona

Battle of Apache Pass, Arizona, July 15, 1862

Union: 1 co., 1st Calif. Inf., Capt. Thomas Roberts; Regt. Battery, 1 section, 1st Calif. Inf., Lt. W. A. Thompson; 1 squadron, Co. B, 2d Calif. Cav., Capt. J. C. Cremony (inactive), total, 126 men; effective total, 102 men, under Capt. Roberts.

Indian: Mimbreno Apache, Mangas Coloradas; Chiricahua Apache, Cochise. Total, ?

Losses: Union, 2 k., 1 w.; Indian, 60 k., ? w.

III—DOCUMENTS

The following documents illustrate points I was unable to resolve completely in the course of my research. These documents have been hitherto unpublished and are presented, with explanations, in the hope that further work can determine their exact significance. I have used them in the body of the work with *probable* inferences as to their meaning, which I supported either by explaining the circumstances under which they were written or by recourse to other documents written later.

A: BAYLOR'S RESIGNATION

In March, 1862, Governor Baylor published an order instructing the Arizona Volunteers of the Sibley Brigade to entice the Apache and all other Indians to parleys, and then to kill all the adults and enslave all the children [*OR* I, L, pt. 1, p. 942; cf. Ch. III, p. 87]. There followed an angry series of letters between General Sibley, usually friendly to the Indians, and Baylor—letters wallowing in vituperation but somehow failing to explain specifically what the anger was all about. Since this outburst of epistles began but a few days after Baylor's order, and ended with his resignation, and since there seems to have been no other reason for the enmity (except for the concomitant fact that Baylor proposed to carry out his extermination with troops nominally subordinate to Sibley, without asking Sibley's permission), the reason for the letters was *probably* Baylor's order.

A second problem is posed by Baylor's resignation. As I state on page 87, "Somehow the two [Sibley and Baylor] shortly reached an understanding," but there is no available evidence to show how. The note on page 87 [footnote 38] explains why Baylor probably chose to submit his resignation to General Sibley rather than General Hebert, or, for that matter, President Davis. Baylor could only resign his military commission through Sibley who, the previous December, had assumed command of all military forces in the Confederate Territory of Arizona. Baylor's appointment as Governor and Indian Commissioner for the Territory had been tendered to him by the Confederate Govern-

Appendices

ment in Richmond (though, admittedly, by doing so the Confederate Government was merely recognizing the *de facto* situation which had existed since August, 1861, and which had been acknowledged by Sibley in December). By submitting his civil resignation to Sibley Baylor probably hoped to show the Commanding General how far he was ready to go if his policies were not supported. Probably, his resignation forced Sibley's hand, and obliged Sibley to come to some sort of an understanding with Baylor.

Mesilla, March 17, 1862

Sir:

I herewith tender my resignation as Colonel and Governor of this Territory, which the General Com. did me the honor to confer upon me.

I should be wanting in self respect were I to [illegible; continue to?] hold a commission under an officer who has shown so palpable a want of confidence in my courage or ability.

I have the honor to be
Very Respectfully &c,
(Signed)   JNO R. BAYLOR

MAJ. A. M. JACKSON   Lt. Col. Com. of T.M.R.
A.A.G., A.N.M.

This letter, written completely in Baylor's hand, is in the Baylor Jacket, National Archives, Washington, D. C.

Major A. M. Jackson was Sibley's Brigade Adjutant.
The abbreviations may be rendered:
    Com. Commanding
    T.M.R. Texas Mounted Rifles
    A.A.G. Assistant Adjutant General [Confederate States Army]
    A.N.M. Army of New Mexico

B: SIBLEY'S ORDERS

The discussion in footnote 17, Ch. 2, page 52 of the work revolves around the issue: What were Sibley's orders from President Davis? His orders were primarily verbal, and he received only one letter to hand-carry to Gen. Earl Van Dorn, Commander of the Department of Texas, to introduce the latter to his plans. This letter is presented here. The reader's attention is brought to the words "certain measures, of which he will advise you upon his arrival." Van Dorn, therefore, learned from Sibley his intentions, and had no written authority with which to restrain Sibley—as far as Van Dorn was concerned, this letter gave Sibley blanket authority to do anything he wished.

The Confederate Invasion of New Mexico and Arizona

Sibley received written authority to establish a civil government in Arizona, to raise a brigade, and to receive the enlistments of United States army deserters. He also received a note authorizing him to carry on a campaign as ordered by President Davis [*OR* I, IV, 93, 141]. Where this campaign was to go, and what it was to accomplish, was not in writing.

The text of the Confederate War Department's letter to Van Dorn appears below:

Adj'n & Insp'r Generals Office
Richmond Va., July 9th 1861

General

General H. H. Sibley under instructions from the President is to proceed to Texas, there to carry out, in concert with yourself, certain measures, of which he will advise you upon his arrival at San Antonio—It is desired that you will extend every facility to General Sibley in successfully carrying out his instructions, supplying as far as possible, the materiel for the armament & equipment of his command, and such needful supplies as he may require from the different departments under your control.

I Am Sir Resply
Y'r. Obd't Ser't

(Signed)   S. COOPER
A.&.I.G.

To
Brig Genl. Earl Van Dorn
Comd'g. San Antonio
          Texas

This letter is written in the handwriting of an unidentified clerk, but the signature is that of General Samuel Cooper, the Adjutant and Inspector General of the Confederate Army. (General Cooper held a position equivalent to that of a modern Chief of Staff. Until General Robert E. Lee's appointment as Commander-in-Chief of the Confederate army in February, 1865, Cooper was the ranking general in the Southern Army, though, being 70 years of age, he never saw field service.)

This letter is in the Sibley Jacket, National Archives, Washington, D. C.

Lines with excessive abbreviations may be rendered:
Adj'n & Insp'r Generals Office: Adjutant and Inspector General's Office.
I Am Sir Resply Y'r. Obd't Ser't: I am, Sir, respectfully, your obedient servant.
A.&.I.G.: Adjutant and Inspector General (C.S.A.).

BIBLIOGRAPHY

Primary Unpublished

CHIVINGTON, JOHN, MAJOR, U. S. A. "The First Colorado Regiment," from the Bancroft *MSS*, Typewritten copy. Museum of New Mexico Library Vertical File, Santa Fe, 1884.

Collections of Private Military Papers (Jackets), Old Army Records Department, Room 8-w, National Archives, Washington, D.C. Includes the "Jackets" of:

    Lt. Col. John R. Baylor, C.S.A.
    Col. Edward R. S. Canby, U.S.A.
    Col. James H. Carleton, U.S.A.
    Col. Christopher ("Kit") Carson, U.S.A.
    Col. John H. Chivington, U.S.A.
    Col. Thomas Green, C.S.A.
    Brig. Gen. William Wing Loring, C.S.A.
    Maj. Charles S. Pyron, C.S.A.
    Col. John Reily, C.S.A.
    Lt. Col. Benjamin Roberts, U.S.A.
    Col. William R. Scurry, C.S.A.
    Brig. Gen. Henry H. Sibley, C.S.A.
    Col. John B. Slough, U.S.A.
    Col. William Steele, C.S.A.
    Maj. Gen. Earl Van Dorn, C.S.A.

FARMER, J. E., PRIVATE, C.S.A. "Autobiography," typewritten copy. Museum of New Mexico Library Vertical File, Santa Fe. No date.

HANNA, EBENEZER, PRIVATE, C.S.A. Journal, February 10-March 27, 1862. *MS* in the Texas State Library, Austin.

NORVELL, STEVENS T., Military Order of the Loyal Legion of the United States. Commandery of the District of Columbia. War papers 45. "New

Mexico in the Civil War" (Read at the Stated Meeting of January 7th, 1903). Museum of New Mexico Library Vertical File, Santa Fe.

Regimental Muster Rolls and Records of Events, *MS* Books in the Old Army Records Department, Room 8-w, National Archives, Washington, D. C.

The following units are represented:

1st California Cavalry, U.S.A.
1st California Volunteer Infantry, U.S.A.
1st Colorado Volunteer Infantry, U.S.A.
1st New Mexico Volunteer Infantry, U.S.A.
1st Texas Artillery, Battery B, C.S.A.
1st United States Cavalry
2d California Cavalry, U.S.A.
2d Colorado Volunteer Infantry, U.S.A.
2d New Mexico Volunteer Infantry, U.S.A.
2d Texas Mounted Volunteers, C.S.A.
2d United States Mounted Rifles
3d United States Cavalry
4th Texas Mounted Volunteers, C.S.A.
5th New Mexico Volunteer Infantry, U.S.A.
5th Texas Mounted Volunteers, C.S.A.
5th United States Infantry
7th Texas Mounted Volunteers, C.S.A.
7th United States Infantry
10th United States Infantry
15th United States Infantry

WRIGHT, H. C. PRIVATE, C.S.A. Letter to Tom Greer, Private, C.S.A., September 7th, 1927. *MS* in the Museum of New Mexico Library Vertical File, Santa Fe.

Secondary Unpublished

BRANNON, GRACE. "Battle of Glorieta." Typewritten copy, Museum of New Mexico Library Vertical File, Santa Fe, 1935.

NORBY, CHARLES H. "The West in the Civil War Decade." Extracts from a Doctoral Dissertation, History Department, University of Iowa, 1935. In the Jefferson Room, Library of Congress Annex, Washington, D. C.

STUART, W. S. "The Battle of Glorieta." Typewritten copy, Museum of New Mexico Library Vertical File, Santa Fe, 1933.

Primary Published—Books

HOLLISTER, OVANDO J., PRIVATE, U.S.A. *Boldly They Rode,* 2d ed. Lakewood, Colo.: The Golden Press, 1949.

McKEE, JAMES C., CAPTAIN, U.S.A. *Narrative of the Surrender of a Command of the U.S. Forces at Fort Fillmore, N.M.* New York, pub. by the author. 1881.

Bibliography

NOEL, THEOPHILUS, PRIVATE, C.S.A. *Autobiography and Reminiscences.* Chicago: Theo. Noel Co. 1904.

PETTIS, GEORGE H., BREVET CAPTAIN, U.S.A. *The California Column, its Campaigns and Services in New Mexico, Arizona and Texas.* Santa Fe: New Mexico Historical Society Papers, No. 11, 1908.

ROWLAND, DUNBAR, ed. *Jefferson Davis, Constitutionalist, His Letters, Papers and Speeches,* Vol. V of 10. Jackson: Mississippi Department of Archives and History. 1923.

WHITFORD, WILLIAM C., PRIVATE, U.S.A. *Colorado Volunteers in the Civil War; The New Mexican Campaign in 1862.* Denver: The State Historical and Natural History Society. 1906.

Primary Published—Articles

ANDERSON, LATHAM, BREVET BRIGADIER-GENERAL, U.S.A. "Canby's Services in the New Mexican Campaign," *Battles and Leaders of the Civil War,* II (1887), 697-699.

BELL, JAMES McC., LIEUTENANT, U.S.A. "The Battle of Val Verde," ed. by Col. M. L. Crimmins, *New Mexico Historical Review,* VII (1932) 348-352.

DARROW, MRS. CAROLINE BALDWIN. "Recollections of the Twiggs Surrender," *Battles and Leaders of the Civil War,* I (1887), 33-39.

EVANS, A. W., LIEUTENANT-COLONEL, U.S.A. "Canby at Valverde," *Battles and Leaders of the Civil War,* II (1887), 699-700.

PETTIS, GEORGE H., BREVET CAPTAIN, U.S.A. "The Confederate Invasion of New Mexico and Arizona," *Battles and Leaders of the Civil War,* II (1887), 103-111.

SMITH, HANK, PRIVATE, C.S.A. "With the Confederates in New Mexico During the Civil War," *Panhandle-Plains Historical Review,* II (1929), 67-97.

TEEL, TREVANION T., CAPTAIN, C.S.A. "Sibley's New Mexican Campaign—Its Objects and the Causes of its Failure," *Battles and Leaders of the Civil War,* II, (1887), p. 700.

Primary Published—Newspapers

DOWNING, JACOB, CAPTAIN, U.S.A., and HOWLAND, JOHN D., PRIVATE, U.S.A. "On Gory Field Glorieta Heights." *Santa Fe New Mexican,* August 6, 7, 8, 1906.

Mesilla (New Mexico) *Times,* May 11, 1861; September 29, 1861.

New York Herald, March 17, 1862.

ROE, LEWIS F., PRIVATE, U.S.A. "With Canby at Valverde, N. M." *The National Tribune* (Washington, D. C.), November 3, 1910.

Sacramento (California) *Union,* May 23, 1862; May 31, 1862.

San Antonio Herald (Texas), June 7, 1862; June 21, 1862; August 9, 1862.

The Confederate Invasion of New Mexico and Arizona

Santa Fe Gazette, October 7, 1865; April 26, 1862.

Santa Fe New Mexican, June 24, 1864; August 11, 1865.

SEAY, ROBERT T., PRIVATE, C.S.A. "Incidents of Glorieta Battle . . ." *Santa Fe New Mexican,* August 13, 1906.

Texas State Gazette (Austin), February 15, 1862.

Primary Published—Official Records

Congress of the Confederate States of America. *Official Reports of Battles, Published by Order of The Confederate Congress at Richmond.* New York: Charles B. Richardson. 1863.

Congress of the United States of America. *Report of the Joint Committee on the Conduct of the War,* vol. III of 5. Washington, Government Printing Office. 1863.

The War of the Rebellion: A Compilation of the Official Records of The Union and Confederate Armies. Series I, vols. I, III, IV, VIII, IX, X, XV, XXV, L (parts 1 and 2); Series IV, vol. I (of 70 vols. in 128 books). Washington: Government Printing Office, 1880-1901.

Secondary Published—Books

BANCROFT, HUBERT H. *History of Arizona and New Mexico,* vol. XVII of Bancroft's Works. San Francisco: The History Company. 1889.

EVANS, CLEMENT A., GENERAL, C.S.A. *Confederate Military History.* Atlanta: Confederate Publishing Company, 1889.

HUNT, AURORA. *The Army of the Pacific.* Glendale Calif.: Arthur H. Clark Co. 1951.

MILLER, FRANCIS T., ED. *Photographic History of the Civil War,* vols. I and X of 10. New York: Review of Reviews Co. 1911.

MONAGHAN, JAY. *Civil War on the Western Border.* Boston: Little, Brown and Co., 1955.

TWITCHELL, RALPH E. *The Leading Facts of New Mexican History.* Cedar Rapids, Iowa: Torch Press. 1912.

WELLMAN, PAUL I. *Glory, God and Gold.* Mainstream of America Series, ed. by Lewis Gannett. Garden City, N. Y.: Doubleday & Co., 1954.

Secondary Published—Pamphlet

HARRIS, GERTRUDE. *A Tale of Men Who Knew Not Fear.* San Antonio: Alamo Printing Press. 1935.

Secondary Published—Articles

CLENDENEN, CLARENCE C. "General James Henry Carleton," *New Mexico Historical Review,* XXX (1955), 23-42.

Appendices

CRIMMINS, M. L. COLONEL, U. S. A. "Fort Fillmore," *New Mexico Historical Review*, VI (1931), 327-333.

DONNELL, F. S. "The Confederate Territory of Arizona." *New Mexico Historical Review*, XVII (1942), 148-163.

HOWELL, D. S. "Along the Texas Frontier During the Civil War," *West Texas Historical Association Yearbook*, XIII (1937), 89-95.

HUNSAKER, WILLIAM J. "Lansford W. Hastings' Project for the Invasion and Conquest of Arizona and New Mexico for the Southern Confederacy," *Arizona Historical Review*, VI (1931-2), 5-12.

RIPPY, J. FRED. "Mexican Projects of the Confederates." *Southwestern Historical Quarterly*, XXII (1918), 291-317.

RODGERS, JUDGE ROBERT L. "The Confederate States Organized Arizona in 1862," *Southern Historical Society Papers*, XXVIII (1900), 222-227.

SANTEE, J. F. "The Battle of La Glorieta Pass," *New Mexico Historical Review*, VI (1931), 66-75.

TITTMAN, EDWARD D. "The Exploitation of Treason," *New Mexico Historical Review*, IV (1929), 128-145.

TWITCHELL, RALPH E. "The Confederate Invasion of New Mexico, Part I." *Old Santa Fe*, III (1916, 5-43).

WALDRIP, WILLIAM I. "New Mexico During the Civil War," *New Mexico Historical Review*, XXVIII (1953), 168-182; 251-290.

WALKER, CHARLES S. "Confederate Government in Dona Ana County," *New Mexico Historical Review*, VI (1931), 253-302.

WALKER, CHARLES S. "Causes of the Confederate Invasion of New Mexico," *New Mexico Historical Review*, VIII (1933), 76-97.

WATFORD, W. H. "Confederate Western Ambitions," *Southwestern Historical Quarterly*, XLIV (1940), 161-187.

WATFORD, W. H. "The Far-Western Wing of the Rebellion, 1861-1865," *California Historical Society Quarterly*, XXXIV (1955), 125-148.

WYLLYS, RUFUS K. "Arizona and the Civil War," *Arizona Highways*, XXVII (1951), 34-39.

Secondary Published—Newspaper

CROCCHIOLA, REV. STANLEY. "Albuquerque was made Headquarters of Confederates in Second War Year." *Santa Fe Register* (N. M.), November 3, 1950.

(NOTE: In addition to the works which, in the original or in photographic or typewritten reproductions, have been examined and are cited here, a number of textbook and/or popular histories of New Mexico and Arizona carry a few remarks or pages regarding the campaign. Twitchell's book, cited above, is the only one of these to present new information.)

INDEX

Numerals indicate pages on which subjects are discussed, though the full name or description of the subjects may not appear on all pages cited. For instance, where prior context indicates that "Confederates" refers only to a particular Regiment in the text, this index cites the concerned pages after the Regimental designation.

The initial military grade following names indicates the grade held by individuals during the major portion of the New Mexican campaign. Subsequent parenthesized ranks designate later promotions or drastic changes in military status.

Index

Index

Mexican Government: 59, 61, 62, 79
Mexicans, Pre-Columbian: 91
Military Department of Kansas, U.S.A.: 81
Military Department of Texas, C.S.A.: 56
Military Department of the Pacific, U.S.A.: 40
Military Department of the Trans-Mississippi, C.S.A.: 77
Military District of East Texas, C.S.A.: 24
Military District of New Mexico, U.S.A.: 128
Military District of Southern California, U.S.A.: 42
Military District of West Texas, C.S.A.: 24
Miller, M. D.: 59
Mines, 78, 78n
Mineral Wealth: 48
Missouri: 27, 28, 39, 59
Modoc Jack: 77
Money, Confederate: 48, 58, 108
Money, Federal: 48
Montgomery, Ala.: 23
Moody, W. G.: 80, 80n
Moore, I., Capt., U.S.A.: 36
Mormons: 46, 50, 50n
Mortimer, —, Capt., U.S.A.: 68
Mountain Meadow Massacre: 50n
Mutiny: 65, 73, 105, 111, 113, 133

Navajo (See also: Indians): 65, 106, 119, 124, 129
Nevada: 48, 48n, 64
New Mexico Territory: 25, 27, 27n, 28, 43, 52
New Mexico Volunteers (See also: Regimental Designations and Commanders' Names): 37, 40, 40n, 53, 65, 67, 68, 71, 73, 75, 83, 84, 85n, 106, 107, 108, 109, 111, 114, 118, 119n
Noel, T., Pvt., C.S.A.: 60, 79, 86, 117
Northern Overland Mail Route: 42
Northwest Ordinance of 1787: 62
Nueva León (Mexican State): 47, 81

Ochiltree, T., Lt., C.S.A.: 57
Ortiz, Rev. —,: 104
Owing, L. S., "Governor of Arizona,": 27n

Panama: 55
Paroles: 35
Paul, G. R., Lt. Col., U.S.A. (Col., U.S.A.): 40, 83, 84, 84n, 89, 107, 111
Pawnee (See also: Indians): 60n
Pecos River: 39, 40, 91
Pelham, W., Confederate States Governor of New Mexico: 88
Peninsular Campaign: 52n
Peons, New Mexican: 53, 58
Peralta, N. M. (See also: Battle of Peralta): 109, 111, 114, 115, 133
Pesqueira, Don I., Governor of Sonora: 79, 80, 80n, 81
Phillips, J., Capt., C.S.A.
Picacho, N. M.: 36
Picacho Pass, Ariz.: 121, 123
Pickett, J., Confederate States Minister to Mexico: 47, 48, 48n
Pigeon's Ranch, N. M.: 92, 92n, 93, 95, 97, 101, 102, 104, 105
Pima Indians (See also: Indians): 78, 79, 120, 121, 123
Pino, M., Col., U.S.A.: 38, 67, 71, 73, 75
Pneumonia: 62
Pony Express: 29n
Price, S., Maj. Gen., C.S.A.: 39n
Pyron, C. S., Maj., C.S.A. (Lt. Col., C.S.A.): 64, 68, 68n, 69n, 71, 73, 87, 88, 89, 92, 93, 95, 96, 97, 97n, 99, 105, 109

Quaker Guns: 76
Quartermaster Stores: 64, 86, 88
Quinterro, J. A.: 43, 43n

Ragnet, H., Maj., C.S.A.: 56, 68, 69, 72, 73, 97, 99
Randolph, G. W., Confederate States Secretary of War: 130
Rations: 76, 85, 88, 110, 113, 118, 132
Reagan, J. H., Confederate States Postmaster General: 43n, 61

Index

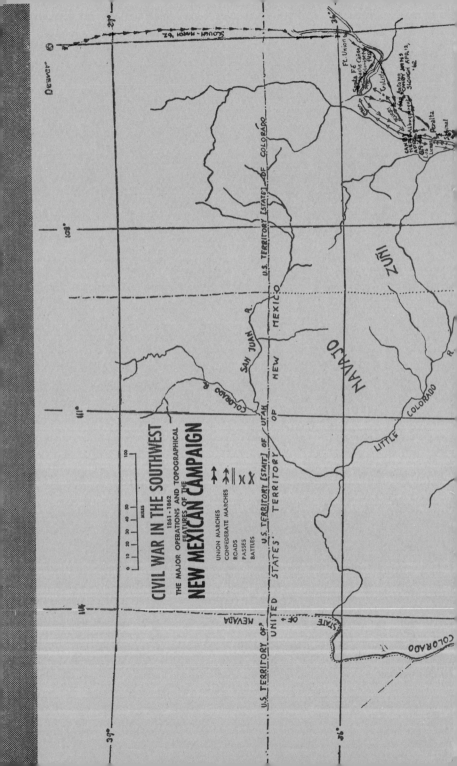

CIVIL WAR IN THE SOUTHWEST
1861 - 1862
THE MAJOR OPERATIONS AND TOPOGRAPHICAL FEATURES OF THE
NEW MEXICAN CAMPAIGN

UNION MARCHES
CONFEDERATE MARCHES
ROADS
PASSES
BATTLES

MILES
0 10 20 30 40 50 100

Denver

Slough - March '62

Ft. Union
Santa Fé
Glorieta
Pigeon's Ranch
Apache Canon
Fort Union
Pecos R.
Albuquerque
Valverde Feb. 21
Peralta
Socorro
Fort Craig
Las Cruces

SAN JUAN R.
COLORADO R.
LITTLE COLORADO R.

NAVAJO
ZUÑI

U.S. TERRITORY [STATE] OF COLORADO
U.S. TERRITORY [STATE] OF UTAH
TERRITORY OF NEW MEXICO

U.S. TERRITORY OF NEVADA
UNITED STATES OF
STATE OF COLORADO